T0303142

Acquisition and Competition Strategy Options for the DD(X)

The U.S. Navy's 21st Century Destroyer

John F. Schank, Giles K. Smith, John Birkler, Brien Alkire,
Michael Boito, Gordon Lee, Rajkumar Raman, John Ablard

Prepared for the U.S. Navy

 NATIONAL DEFENSE RESEARCH INSTITUTE

The research described in this report was prepared for the U.S. Navy. The research was conducted in the RAND National Defense Research Institute, a federally funded research and development center sponsored by the OSD, the Joint Staff, the Unified Combatant Commands, the Department of the Navy, the Marine Corps, the defense agencies, and the defense Intelligence Community under Contract DASW01-01-C-0004.

Library of Congress Cataloging-in-Publication Data

Acquisition and competition strategy options for the DD(X) : the U.S. Navy's 21st
  century destroyer / John F. Schank ... [et al.].
    p. cm.
  "MG-259/1."
  Includes bibliographical references.
  ISBN 0-8330-3870-2 (pbk. : alk. paper)
  1. United States. Navy—Procurement. 2. Defense contracts—United States.
  3. Destroyers (Warships)—United States. I. Schank, John F. (John Frederic), 1946–

VC263.A796 2006
359.8'3540687—dc22

                                                                    2005029955

The RAND Corporation is a nonprofit research organization providing objective analysis and effective solutions that address the challenges facing the public and private sectors around the world. RAND's publications do not necessarily reflect the opinions of its research clients and sponsors.

RAND® is a registered trademark.

Cover design by Stephen Bloodsworth
Cover image courtesy of the DD(X) National Team

Published 2006 by the RAND Corporation
1776 Main Street, P.O. Box 2138, Santa Monica, CA 90407-2138
1200 South Hayes Street, Arlington, VA 22202-5050
201 North Craig Street, Suite 202, Pittsburgh, PA 15213-1516
RAND URL: http://www.rand.org/
To order RAND documents or to obtain additional information, contact
Distribution Services: Telephone: (310) 451-7002;
Fax: (310) 451-6915; Email: order@rand.org

Preface

In 1994, the U.S. Navy initiated a program to transform America's surface combatant fleet by developing a new family of ships intended to project power more rapidly, wage war more effectively, and operate less expensively, compared with vessels currently in the fleet.

The centerpiece of this new family of ships will be a destroyer, currently designated DD(X). After several years of study of alternative system concepts, design proposals for the DD(X) were solicited from two industry teams. In April 2002, one of those teams, led by Northrop Grumman Ship Systems (NGSS), was selected winner of the competition and awarded a $2.9 billion contract to manage a three-year risk-reduction phase and to act as the lead design agent for the program. The Navy also specified that the shipyard member of the other industry team, Bath Iron Works (BIW), should participate in ship design and production activities. This effort to ensure continued existence of two shipyards capable of developing and producing surface combatants had important consequences in the Navy's ability to beneficially use competition during development and production of the DD(X).

Detail design of the lead ships is now scheduled to start in 2006, with fabrication commencing in 2007. Acquisition and contracting decisions that the Navy makes during that next phase of the program will have important implications not only for the U.S. industrial base involved in manufacturing and equipping surface combatants but for options available in subsequent phases of the DD(X) acquisition.

In 2003, the Navy asked the RAND Corporation to evaluate the advantages and disadvantages of different acquisition and contracting strategies that defense officials could employ on the DD(X) program to achieve three objectives: make the best use of competition throughout the detail design and production; maintain a strong industrial base capable of building surface combatants; and achieve program cost, schedule, and performance objectives. Over the six-month duration of this study, RAND sought to identify strategies designed to achieve those objectives.

RAND conducted and documented this research before U.S. defense officials significantly changed the program in 2005, cutting the total number of ships that the Navy would acquire by 50 percent or more and changing the structure and organization of its management. Thus, this study is a snapshot of the program as it existed in 2003 and 2004, before those changes were put in place. Nevertheless, this report should be of special interest to the Navy, to uniformed and civilian decisionmakers involved in weapon systems acquisitions, and to companies involved in designing and manufacturing warships.

This research was sponsored by the DD(X) Program Manager in the Program Executive Office Ships, Department of the Navy, and conducted within the Acquisition and Technology Policy Center of the RAND National Defense Research Institute (NDRI), a federally funded research and development center sponsored by the Office of the Secretary of Defense, the Joint Staff, the Unified Combatant Commands, the Department of the Navy, the Marine Corps, the defense agencies, and the defense Intelligence Community.

For more information on RAND's Acquisition and Technology Policy Center, contact the Director, Phil Antón. He can be reached by e-mail at atpc-director@rand.org; by phone at 310-393-0411, extension 7798; or by mail at the RAND Corporation, 1776 Main Street, Santa Monica, California 90407-2138). More information about RAND is available at www.rand.org.

Contents

Figures

Tables

Summary

In 1994, the U.S. Navy initiated a program to transform America's surface combatant fleet by developing a new family of ships. These new ships—equipped with a range of state-of-the-art hull, propulsion, weapons, electronics, and communications technologies—were designed to enable the Navy to project power more rapidly, wage war more effectively, and operate less expensively, compared with vessels currently in the fleet.

To implement this transformation effort, the Navy has prepared an acquisition plan that will extend over the next two decades. The acquisition plan in place at the time we conducted and documented this study aimed to procure and place into service the entire family of new ships, consisting of up to 24 destroyers, along with an undetermined number of cruisers and smaller vessels for littoral operations, by about 2025. As explained in Chapter Six, that plan was revised significantly in 2005, scaling back the Navy's acquisition to between eight and 12 of the new destroyers.

The destroyer—currently designated DD(X)—will be the centerpiece of this new family. Navy planners envision that the DD(X) will be a multimission surface combatant capable of bringing offensive, distributed, and precision firepower at long range in support of forces ashore. At the time of our study, the Navy planned to procure the first DD(X) in 2005 and to have that vessel delivered into service in 2011. According to the revised, smaller acquisition plan announced in 2005, those procurement and delivery dates will be postponed by a year.

The Challenge

The DD(X) program is approaching a key decision point in the Department of Defense (DoD) acquisition process. Starting in mid-1998, two competitive industry teams conducted design studies during Phases I and II of the program. In April 2002, the team led by Northrop Grumman Ship Systems (NGSS) and including Raytheon Systems Co. was selected as winner of that competition and placed under contract to perform a three-year technology development and maturation effort (Phase III). Upon completion of Phase III, scheduled for the first half of CY 2005, the program will be ready to enter Phase IV. At that time a Milestone B review will be performed and the Navy will negotiate contracts for the detail design of the ship and warfare system and construction and test of the lead ship.

In most major system acquisitions, completing a Milestone B review would result in the Navy selecting a single prime contractor and authorizing it to perform the program's remaining development and production efforts. However, the DD(X) program differs from that traditional process in two important ways. First, as noted above, a winner of the design rivalry was selected in mid-2002 and awarded nearly $3 billion for a three-year period of technology development and maturation *before* starting detail design and lead ship construction. Second, the Acquisition Strategy approved at the beginning of Phase III included the statement, "The Navy intends to have competition in detail design and ship construction throughout the production period" (*DD[X] Land Attack Destroyer Single Acquisition Management Plan,* Revision D, November 27, 2001, p. 18).

Currently, only two shipyards (Bath Iron Works and NGSS/Ingalls) have a demonstrated capability of building DD(X)-class surface combatants. Thus, in Phase IV of the DD(X) program the Navy faces a range of objectives that are not always internally consistent: make the best use of competition throughout detail design and production; maintain a strong industrial base capable of building surface combatants; and achieve program cost, schedule, and performance objectives.

The decisions the DD(X) Program Office makes with respect to these issues will shape the future of the program. Recognizing the importance of these decisions, the Navy in 2003 tasked RAND to evaluate the advantages and disadvantages of different acquisition and contracting strategies that defense officials could employ on the DD(X) program. Over the six-month duration of this study, RAND sought to identify strategies that would increase the likelihood that the Navy would achieve its full range of program objectives.

How the Challenge Was Examined

We pursued this evaluation by asking three questions:

- What DD(X) program tasks might be appropriate to compete in the future?
- How should the DD(X) program be organized to best support the objective of ensuring a continued presence of a strong ship-building industrial base for surface combatants, at minimum cost to the Navy?
- What are the relative advantages and risks of alternative con-tracting methods for the various tasks involved in Phase IV?

We examined the issue of how best to employ competition by first laying out a rich set of options, some employing head-to-head competition at various points during Phase IV and others resorting to directed buys. Each option was then examined by drawing on experi-ence from past major defense acquisition programs and estimating the likely balance of costs and benefits resulting from each option. While the results are largely subjective, they are based on a substantial his-tory of how competition has worked out in a variety of earlier acquisi-tion programs.

Effects of the DD(X) program on the shipbuilding industrial base were examined by modeling the supply and demand for shipyard labor under each of several options for distributing the work among the two shipyards and for scheduling the work across calendar time.

While the effects of those different business profiles on the continuing viability of the firms could not be deduced with great precision, the analysis did provide useful insights.

Finally, several different contracting strategies were examined in terms of how they would accommodate the particular objectives and constraints of the DD(X) program, and conclusions were drawn based on outcomes of similar programs and contract strategies in the past.

Results of the Study

We came to three overarching conclusions.

Neither design rivalry for system configuration nor price competition for production of the DD(X)'s ship systems and warfare systems appears practical during the initial portions of Phase IV. An extended design rivalry was conducted during Phases I and II of the program. Reopening that design rivalry after three years and about $3 billion invested in refinement and risk reduction would entail significant costs in time and dollars, and we could see no reasonable basis for expecting corresponding benefits in either cost of the detail design process or quality of the detail design product.

Price competition has been generally difficult to achieve in production of military ship systems. Quantities are relatively small, and costs of starting and sustaining a second producer are relatively large, thus making direct cost competition impractical in most cases. There has been some suggestions of benefits from competition in production of ships with long production runs.[1] However, achievement of similar results in DD(X) production would be severely limited by the Navy's stated policy of sustaining both shipyards as viable business entities, and by the desire for cooperation between the shipyards during detail design. On balance, we conclude that price competition

---

[1] This issue is examined in Appendix B. While Navy program managers believe they have achieved some benefits from competition in such programs as the DDG 51 class, it is not possible to demonstrate from procurement records that a true price reduction was achieved.

for the early phases of ship production is impractical. Similarly, price competition for warfare system production will be impractical during at least the initial production because of the likely evolution of the design and very short production runs for any particular configuration.

The currently projected schedule of detail ship design and construction together with the plan to distribute business equally to both shipyards should provide enough business to sustain both shipyards as viable competitors for future surface combatant programs. While the projected overall *level* of business from the DD(X) program appears sufficient to sustain both shipyards at a level of activity near that of the 1990s, that conclusion is subject to two important caveats. One is that ship design and construction schedule must not be allowed to slip very much. The DD(X) Program Office's current plan postulates an even distribution of ships to the two shipyards, with the lead ship going to NGSS, the second ship to BIW, and then alternating allocation of ships until the end of the production run. Under the acquisition plan in place at the time we conducted our research, production of the first DD(X) was scheduled to start in August 2007. That was already too late to permit a smooth transition from other work to DD(X) production at either shipyard, and consequently each shipyard will experience some turbulence in demand for shipyard labor, with consequent increase in cost. While those transients appear manageable (albeit at some cost), the history of major weapon development programs shows that schedules projected before start of final design and initial ship construction are rarely achieved, whether because of technical or funding problems. Our analysis showed that delays of even one year, particularly for the first ship to be constructed at BIW, could lead to serious levels of turbulence in demand for ship construction labor and consequent increased cost of discharging, hiring, and training workers. Greater delays could endanger the objective of supporting both shipyards or demand other actions to support the production labor pool at that shipyard during the transition.

We found that changing the allocation of work between the shipyards would not offer unencumbered benefits. We estimated that shifting the allocation to as much as 75 percent to one shipyard or the other would be near the limit of practicality in terms of sustaining both shipyards as viable commercial concerns. Within that range, each shift might smooth the labor demand in one shipyard but worsen it in the other. No distribution uniformly stood out as the best alternative.

The second caveat to the "industrial base support" conclusion is that both shipyards must receive substantial levels of ship design work to sustain their technical staffs. That might pose a challenge to the Navy in creating a contracting and management strategy for the detail design and early ship construction period in the DD(X) program. That challenge is discussed below.

The presence of three major producers (two shipyards and a mission equipment producer/integrator) in the program and the presence of both design and production tasks to be performed in Phase IV suggest a mix of contracting strategies.

We examined several different contracting methods that could be applied to Phase IV, with special attention to how each method would affect the balance of Navy management workload and Navy opportunities to exercise close control over the industry members.

- One option would call for the Navy to contract individually with each major member of the industry team now involved with the DD(X): each shipyard and the warfare system producer. That would require the Navy to manage the total system integration during detail design and then to provide the warfare system as government-furnished equipment (GFE) to each shipyard during production. We deemed that level of Navy involvement to be inconsistent with recent trends in Navy management staffing and with Navy policy.

- A second group of options would require a single industry agent to contract with the Navy for full management of detail design and subsequent production. That single agent could be one of the firms now developing the DD(X) or a consortium of the several major participants. If one contractor served as the single agent throughout construction, the inherent competitive posture between the two shipyards could pose problems in administration. A preferred strategy would be to encourage the key firms to create a consortium, with the appropriate interfirm agreements and protocols worked out in advance to the greatest extent possible. The current agreement between Newport News Shipyard and Electric Boat for production of the *Virginia*-class submarine appears to be a useful model.

- A third option would be to use different contracting models for different tasks and phases of the project. Use of a single prime to manage detail design and final system integration has powerful advantages of focusing authority for managing that technically demanding task. Conversely, the Navy could better control the production process by contracting directly with the shipyards, thus retaining an opportunity to inject some level of competition into the later stages of that production. Such a multistage contracting strategy does not have a well-developed history or proven set of practices and must be approached with care.

We concluded that the third option is most likely to provide an effective contract structure for managing Phase IV of the DD(X) program.

Acknowledgments

This research could not have been accomplished without the assistance of many individuals. Captain Charles Goddard, DD(X) program manager, supported and encouraged the work. Numerous individuals in the DD(X) program office offered information, advice, and assistance. F. Scott DiLisio, deputy program manager; Leon Godfrey; and Clayton Aherns were especially helpful, providing background on the DD(X) program and offering constructive criticism of interim findings and documentation. Jill Boward of the Cost Engineering and Industrial Analysis Division of Naval Sea Systems Command provided cost data that were helpful in evaluating the various acquisition options. If we were to single out one individual who supported us in extraordinary ways, it would be Michael Gray who provided data and information and facilitated our interactions with multiple organizations.

Captain David Lewis, DDG 51 program manager, and Randy Fortune, deputy program manager, shared their knowledge and expertise on the DDG 51 program. Dirk Lesko, Jerry Steiner, Andrew Bond and Nick Nichols from Bath Iron Works and Don Perkins from Northrop Grumman Ship Systems shared their time and information with us on the DD(X) program.

RAND colleagues Jeff Drezner and Irv Blickstein offered many constructive comments on earlier drafts that helped strengthen the final report. Debbie Peetz of RAND provided her usual excellent support, contributing a variety of information on the DDG 51 and the DD(X) programs. We are additionally indebted to Joan Myers for her deft assistance in organizing and formatting the many drafts and to Dan Sheehan for his editing.

Abbreviations

AFSS	Autonomic fire suppression system
AGS	Advanced gun system
BIW	Bath Iron Works
CG	Guided-missile cruiser class
DCP	Decision coordinating paper
DD	Destroyer class
DD(X)	Destroyer next-generation
DMRB	Destroyer Management Review Board
DoD	Department of Defense
EDM	Engineering Development Model
FFG	Guided-missile frigate class
FOUO	For official use only
FPI	Fixed-price incentive
FTE	Full-time equivalent
GAO	General Accounting Office
GFE	Government-furnished equipment
GFI	Government-furnished information
IPS	Integrated power system
IUSW	Integrated undersea warfare
LHA(R)	Amphibious assault ship replacement

MNS	Mission need statement
NGSS	Northrop Grumman Ship Systems
NSC	National Security Cutter
OMB	Office of Management and Budget
ORD	Operational requirements document
PPBS	Planning, Programming, and Budgeting System
PRO	Profit related to offer
PVLS	Peripheral vertical launch system
RFP	Request for proposal
SAMP	Single Acquisition Management Plan
SCN	Shipbuilding and conversion, Navy
TDP	Technical data package
USN	U.S. Navy
VLS	Vertical launch system

A Note on Terminology

In 2001, the DoD oversight management of major weapon systems, as defined in the DoD 5000-series regulations, was substantially revised, with new procedures and new terminology. Furthermore, some of the terminology used to describe the DD(X) program includes terms that occur in the DoD oversight management process but with different meaning. This can lead to confusion. In the present report the following terms are used:

Milestone 0: This event, a part of the pre-2001 DoD acquisition management process, authorized studies of alternative system concepts to satisfy the identified mission need. The milestone did not signify the start of an acquisition program and did not require formal interface with the Planning, Programming, and Budgeting System (PPBS). In the DD 21 program, this milestone was passed in January 1995.

Milestone I: This event, a part of the pre-2001 DoD acquisition management process, authorized start of a new acquisition program and required that anticipated future expenditures be reflected in the future-year budgets and other PPBS documents. The work authorized by this milestone included design refinement, technology development of critical subsystems, and prototyping when appropriate. In the DD 21 program, this milestone was passed in January 1998.

Milestone B: This event, part of the post-2001 DoD 5000-series regulations, authorizes start of full-scale development and the manufacture of initial units for developmental and operational testing. In the DD(X) program, this milestone will be the first to be passed under the new acquisition management process and is anticipated for the first half of CY 2005.

A further source of possible confusion lies in the use of "phase" to define a period in both the DD(X) Program and the DoD acquisition management process. In this report, the term will be used *only* to depict certain portions of the DD(X) program. Phases I and II were conducted under the original DD 21 program, while Phases III and IV represent portions following program restructuring and renaming as DD(X).

CHAPTER ONE

Introduction

In 1994, the U.S. Navy initiated a program to develop a new family of ships to transform its surface combatant fleet. That program, originally designated the SC 21 program to signify the surface combatants for the twenty-first century, was conceived as including a new destroyer (DD 21 class) and a new cruiser (CG 21 class). The initial focus of the program was to be on developing and procuring the destroyer version, to be followed later by the cruiser version.

Early Navy documents stated that the DD 21 system would provide an advanced level of land attack in support of the ground campaign and contribute to naval, joint, and combined battlespace dominance in littoral operations. The ships would possess the operational flexibility to meet the multimission forward presence and warfighting requirements of the littoral environment and employ self-defense against the threats anticipated for the twenty-first century. The ships would also be capable of taking advantage of, and maintaining the benefits of, the military revolution stimulated by the rapid advances in information and information-related technologies and exploit them through automation and system architectures capable of disseminating information to widely dispersed and dissimilar units to achieve an overall dominant maneuver concept of operations, as outlined in Joint Vision 2010 and concepts for future joint operations.[1]

---

[1] Memorandum from Principal Deputy Assistant Secretary of the Navy (RD&A), June 5, 1998.

The Navy's surface combatant fleet currently consists of four classes—a cruiser class (CG 47), a guided-missile frigate class (FFG 8), and two destroyer classes (DDG 51 and DDG 963)—only one of which (the DDG 51) is still in production. By the end of the present decade, two of the older designs will have been largely retired, and the DDG 51 class will no longer be in production. Thus, the proposed new family of ships will fill important roles of modernizing and transforming the fleet while providing an active production base.

Total production quantities for the new destroyer cannot be predicted with confidence, but the acquisition plan in place at the time we conducted and documented this research suggested about two dozen ships to be delivered between about 2011 and 2022. The contribution of the new class to the surface warfare force over the next couple of decades is depicted in Figure 1.1.[2] Note that this figure does not reflect the 2005 changes to the program that we discuss in Chapter Six.

As reflected in the early planning documents, the SC 21 program was to follow a conventional acquisition process as outlined in the DoD 5000 series of acquisition policy directives. Those plans called for competitive development of design concepts, followed by a source selection for final system development and production, with the winner announced in 2001.

Since the initial formulation in 1994, the program has evolved, reflecting a number of uncertainties, difficulties, and opportunities:

- a rapidly changing threat, and the corresponding desire to incorporate a wide range of new combat capabilities, many of them requiring untested operational employment strategies;
- new technologies offering opportunities for new operational capabilities but also posing new risks; and

---

[2] The retirement of the FFG 8 and the DD 963 classes has not been officially scheduled. For this illustration we estimated that the FFG 8 class will be retired when the currently active ships reach 25 years of service, and the DD 963 class will be retired at 30 years of age. Those estimates are consistent with recent histories for those ship classes but could be modified to meet future needs.

Figure 1.1
Recent Past and Near Future Composition of the Surface Combatant Force

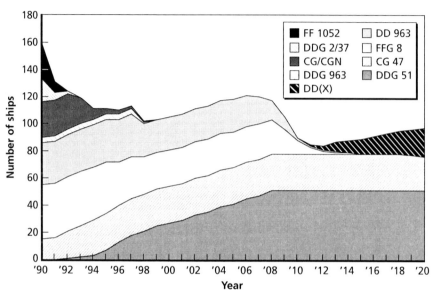

RAND *MG259/1-1.1*

- continuing budget pressure and competition from other Navy shipbuilding needs, as well as other Navy needs, such as aircraft procurement, readiness, and personnel funding.

These forces led to several revisions in the original acquisition plan, with detail design and lead ship construction expected to be authorized in the first half of CY 2005. Those revisions, summarized below, also introduced some new issues and options for subsequent phases of the program. In July 2003, the program manager asked RAND to examine some of those issues, including the best use of competition, the effects of different strategies for sustaining the shipbuilding industry, and the use of alternative contracting methods for future program activities. Results of the RAND analysis were provided to the Navy during the period from mid-October 2003 to early January 2004.

This report describes the issues that RAND addressed, how the analysis was conducted, and the research results.

Program Overview

In January 1998, Jacques Gansler, then Under Secretary of Defense for Acquisition and Technology, issued an Acquisition Decision Memorandum signifying completion of Milestone I[3] for the SC 21 program and authorizing the start of program definition and risk reduction for the DD 21 portion of the program. As described in Navy documents, the program would consist of five phases:

- Phase I: development of the DD 21 system concept designs;
- Phase II: development of initial system designs and smart product models;
- Phase III: completion of system and subsystem design;
- Phase IV: detailed design and construction of the lead ship and subsequent serial production of the remaining ships;
- Phase V: initial engineering and logistics life-cycle support.

It was anticipated that as many as three firms might compete during Phase I. If necessary, a down-select at the end of Phase I would leave two firms competing during Phase II. Another down-select would then award subsequent phases to a single firm. However, that final down-select would not result in a winner-take-all award. The winner would be selected on the basis of a design rivalry, and that winner would become the lead design agent but would not have exclusive right to produce the ship. Only two shipyards, Bath Iron Works (BIW) and Ingalls Shipbuilding Inc., had a demonstrated ability to produce such ships, based on the then-current DDG 51

---

[3] See the "Note on Terminology" on p. xxvii for a description of terminology used to describe portions of the DD 21 program and the DoD acquisition management oversight procedures.

program.[4] The Navy wished to ensure that both shipyards would participate in the DD 21 production program in order to provide cost competition throughout the production phase and be available for competitive sourcing in future programs.

The organization of the DD 21 program was further influenced by a second factor. The combat system, consisting of electronics, communications, fire control, and ordnance, would be substantially more complex and costly than in previous systems, and the integration of those elements with the ship's hull and mechanical and electrical elements would pose new challenges in integration management. In the then-current DDG 51 system, the Aegis combat system was procured separately by the Navy and provided to the shipbuilders as government-furnished equipment (GFE). For the DD 21 system, the Navy wanted industry to be responsible for the entire system-integration task. Neither shipyard was prepared to perform such a task, so it seemed necessary to create a contractual and business relationship that would combine several firms that together would possess the requisite technical and management capabilities.

A draft request for proposal (RFP) for Phase I of the DD 21 program was released to industry for comment and questions in November 1997, but informal discussions indicated that only one bid would be received, from a team consisting of both shipyards and a systems integrator. Such an arrangement would preclude any opportunity for competition between suppliers. After exploring alternatives, the Navy elected to "designate [BIW and Ingalls] as the two DD 21 shipbuilders that would form an alliance for the purpose of establishing two separate teams to competitively develop two robust DD 21 design concepts. Ultimately, the designated shipbuilders will competitively produce the DD 21 ships."[5]

Two industry teams responded, each consisting of a ship builder and a warfare system developer/integrator. One, called the Gold

---

[4] The current status of the shipbuilding industry is described in Chapter Three. The DDG 51 program is described in Appendix A.

[5] Memorandum from Principal Deputy Assistant Secretary of the Navy (RD&A), June 5, 1998.

Team, consisted of Ingalls Shipbuilding Inc. (now NGSS Ingalls Operations) and Raytheon Systems Co., while the other, called the Blue Team, consisted of Bath Iron Works Corp. (BIW) and Lockheed Martin Corp. Those two teams competed throughout Phases I and II. Both phases were conducted under "Other Transaction Authority" (Smith, Drezner, and Lachow, 2002).

The original plan was for Phase II to end in spring 2001, followed by down-select to a single full-service contractor who would complete the system design and construct the lead ship. However, in May 2001 the source selection was held in abeyance pending results of several major studies and reviews of military force structure then being conducted within the Department of Defense. During the intervening period, the two industry teams were instructed to continue design efforts.

In November 2001 the program was restructured and redesignated DD(X). The revised Single Acquisition Management Plan (SAMP) issued in November 2001 describes the change (*DD[X] Land Attack Destroyer Single Acquisition Management Plan*, Revision D, November 27, 2001, Section 4):

> At the completion of Phase II, the plan was to down-select a DD 21 Full Service Contractor to complete the system design as a Single Step to Full Capability approach, construct the first four DD 21 ships (two shipbuilders), and establish the basis of industry's responsibilities for Life Cycle Engineering and Support to the DD 21 class. A Request for Proposals was released in September 2000, with down-select originally planned for Spring 2001 and subsequently extended to June 2001. The DD 21 Source Selection was held in abeyance on 1 May 2001 by the Under Secretary of the Navy pending results of the [Quadrennial Defense Review], OSD Shipbuilding Study and DPG reviews.
>
> [The Under Secretary of Defense for Acquisition, Technology, and Logistics] approved restructuring the DD 21 Program and revising the acquisition strategy on 13 November 2001. The DD 21 Program was redesigned as DD(X), and the program focus was shifted to technology development and maturation,

including robust land-based and at-sea testing of transformational technologies that could be leveraged across multiple ship classes. In conjunction with the DD(X) Phase III technology development contract, the Navy will conduct a spiral design review that permits early Milestone B activities to revalidate [operational requirements document] requirements. The spiral design review will also assess the merits of achieving various levels of capability across a family of multi-mission ships, including a future cruiser, CG(X), and a Littoral Combat Ship (LCS).

The revised acquisition plan also specified that Phase III would include development and testing of ten Engineering Development Models (EDMs) outlined in Table 1.1. These EDMs involve technologies that will be used throughout the ship, as shown in Figure 1.2. Some of the EDMs were included in the Phase II designs, including an advanced gun and reduced manning. However, the system concept outlined in the above statement reflected a much more aggressive effort to incorporate new and innovative technologies into the DD(X) design, making it more responsive to emerging threats and technological opportunities. Thus the intent of Phase III was expanded to incorporate both development and demonstration of advanced concepts, some of which might be used in other new ships, such as the CG(X) and the LCS.

A new RFP for Phase III was issued to the two teams that had been competing during Phases I and II. That solicitation called only for technology development and maturation and did not include options for subsequent ship construction, which was expected to be competitively awarded in the FY 2005 time period.

Table 1.1
Engineering Development Models Addressed in Phase III

Advanced Gun System (AGS)	Integrated Power System (IPS)
Autonomic Fire-Suppression System (AFSC)	Integrated Undersea Warfare System (IUWS)
Dual-Band Radar Suite (DBR)	Infrared Mockups
Hull Form Scale Model	Peripheral Vertical Launching System (PVLS)
Integrated Deckhouse and Apertures	Total Ship Computing Environment

Figure 1.2
Key Elements of the DD(X) System

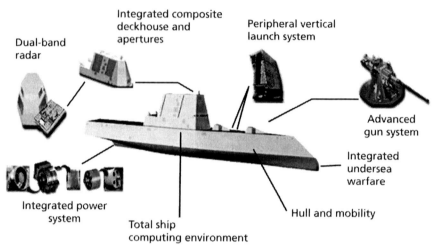

RAND MG259/1-1.2

In April 2002, the Ingalls-Raytheon Gold Team was selected as winner of the competition for Phase III and awarded a three-year contract with a value of approximately $2.9 billion.

At the end of Phase III, it is envisioned that one or more new contracts will be issued for Phase IV that will include detail design of the ship and associated warfare system, production of the lead ship, and production of the second ship at the alternative shipyard. The key events of the resulting program are outlined in Figure 1.3.

Thus, after ten years of planning, design studies, and technology development, the program is approaching a key decision point in the DoD acquisition process: Milestone B, authorizing start of system development and demonstration, which will include detail design of the ship and warfare system and construction and test of the lead ship. At the time we conducted this study, Milestone B review was scheduled for spring 2005. In most major system acquisition programs, the transition across Milestone B involves the final source selection of a single prime contractor that is then authorized to perform the remainder of the development and production process.

Figure 1.3
Key Events in the DD 21/DD(X) Program

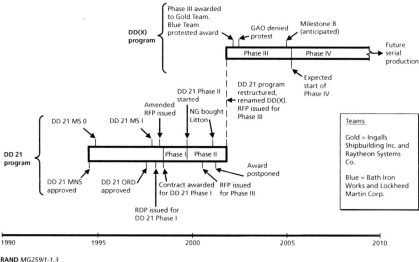

However, the unusual evolution of the DD(X) program, and the special constraints and objectives posed for the next phase, present a complex set of options for managing the remainder of the program. Therefore, the design of an overall acquisition strategy for Phase IV demands careful scrutiny.

Issues for Phase IV

Two aspects of the DD(X) program pose special challenges for the organization and management of Phase IV. One stems from the goal of achieving sustained competition throughout a production phase when there are only two qualified producers and the buyer is publicly committed to keeping both producers in business.[6] The situation becomes especially troublesome when the DD(X) program is expected to constitute the vast majority of the production business at

---

[6] See Memorandum from Principal Deputy Assistant Secretary of the Navy, June 5, 1998.

one or both suppliers. That situation existed throughout the DDG 51 program and is expected to exist throughout the DD(X) program.

The second challenging aspect of the program is to devise a contractual and business relationship that will satisfy two goals: to shift overall system integration management to industry while retaining some capability to achieve competition between shipbuilders and to establish and maintain a substantial degree of synergy and cooperation among the shipyards, the combat system supplier, and the system integrator throughout the detail design and construction of the DD(X) system. How the enabling contractual and business arrangements should be made with the firms is far from obvious.

Research Strategy

The strategy used to examine these two issues was to first decompose the initial issue into two elements: how to achieve competition among suppliers and how to ensure that each shipyard remains a viable business enterprise, but at the lowest cost to the Navy. Each goal was individually examined, while recognizing and accounting for the inherent tensions between the two goals. Building on the results of those two investigations, the third issue of contractual and business arrangements was then examined. That led to the following three research tasks: examining the appropriate use of competition throughout Phase IV, evaluating ways to sustain the industrial base, and exploring contracting strategies for Phase IV.

Examining the Appropriate Use of Competition Throughout Phase IV

In the original design of the DD 21 program, it was envisioned that at the end of Phase II a source selection would be made and the winner would be awarded a contract for further development and production of the system. That plan included a provision that ship construction would be distributed to both shipyards, without specifying how such distribution was to be managed. This was the same practice the Navy had followed in construction of the DDG 51 ships, which had been divided between the same two shipyards, sometimes on the basis of cost competition and sometimes through allocation and other unique contract provisions. A study was made of the DDG

51 acquisition history (reported in Appendix A). Results from that experience were combined with results of numerous other competitive acquisitions and prior surveys of competitive acquisition of weapon systems and components. That body of information provided a basis for estimating the balance of costs and benefits for each of several different ways that competition might be employed in the DD(X) Phase IV circumstances and objectives. Results are described in Chapter Two.

Evaluating Ways to Sustain the Industrial Base

In the past two or three decades, economic forces have led to considerable consolidation in the industry segments that support the national defense establishment. In some segments, including shipbuilding, we are approaching a point where only one firm will be available to provide certain kinds of weapon systems.[7] Thus the Department of Defense is being forced to examine policies that might be employed to ensure continued existence of multiple, competitive firms in certain segments of the military industrial base.

The problem of a shrinking industrial base has become acute in the industry segment that produces destroyers, cruisers, and similar ships that make up a class generally referred to as "surface combatants." Today, only two firms possess current experience and demonstrated capability to develop and produce such ships: BIW and NGSS/Ingalls. From the earliest days of the DD 21/DD(X) program, acquisition plans have reflected a policy to allow both shipyards to participate in production of the DD(X). However, no policy guidance has been given on how to balance the immediate DD(X) program objectives of meeting cost, schedule, and system performance goals with the broader DoD objective of ensuring that a vital and competitive industrial base will support future programs.

Achieving that balance raises a set of questions about how ship production work might be allocated or apportioned to the two shipyards and how such allocations would affect their production costs

---

[7] A similar contraction of the military aircraft industry is studied in Birkler et al. (2003).

and their continuing viability. This issue was examined by modeling the demands for shipyard labor and estimating the cost of providing that labor force under a variety of ship construction and allocation schedules. The analysis led to insights into how the DD(X) ship construction program might be structured to ensure continued viability of both shipbuilders while reducing the consequent costs to the DD(X) program. Results are presented in Chapter Three.

Exploring Contracting Strategies for Phase IV

If the original DD 21 program had proceeded as originally designed, the "competition winner" selected at the end of Phase II would have been designated as a full-service prime, with one or more contracts awarded to it for subsequent activities. That same pattern was followed in awarding a single contract to NGSS for the Phase III risk-reduction and system design activities. It also could be followed for the subsequent Phase IV. However, the unusual history of the program, the mandate to support both shipyards, and the fact that the warfare system producer (Raytheon Systems Co.) would be allocated nearly half the total program funding, led the program office to revisit the question of contract structures. Might there be some other arrangement of contracts that would better serve the Navy in managing Phase IV of the program? Drawing from experience with several different contracting strategies that have been employed in recent ship acquisition programs, we outlined a variety of possible contracting strategies and subjectively estimated their relative advantages and disadvantages. Results are described in Chapter Four.

Organization of the Report

The remainder of this report is divided into three main chapters, following the topical structure of the three issues we examined, as described above. A fifth chapter briefly summarizes our overall results and conclusions. A final chapter adds an epilogue that briefly describes developments affecting the DD(X) program that took place in late 2004 and 2005, long after we had concluded and documented our research. These developments significantly reduced the number of DD(X) ships that the Navy will acquire and altered the structures whereby government and industry will manage the program. Supplementary information on the DDG 51 program history is provided in Appendix A. A survey of competitive strategies and consequences in recent ship acquisition programs appears in Appendix B. The forms used to solicit supporting data from the shipbuilders are presented in Appendix C.

CHAPTER TWO
Applications of Competition in Phase IV

Consolidations in the defense industry and declining defense budgets have made many major defense acquisition programs dependent on one or two sources for crucial systems and subsystems. This dependence has raised concern within DoD and Congress in recent years, with some observers worrying that it has resulted in DoD paying higher prices for less-innovative systems than it would have paid in an arena involving more competitors. Under these conditions, it is important to examine how, and how much, competition can be applied to subsequent phases of the DD(X) program. In this chapter, we first briefly discuss the special characteristics of competition in defense procurement and then examine each of several specific ways that competition could be applied to Phase IV of the DD(X) program.

Defense Acquisitions: Not Business as Usual

Major defense acquisitions are complex and unique and cannot follow typical business practices of price competition. In the typical consumer products market, a buyer examines the available products, requests competitive bids for production from a number of contractors, selects a bid based on a fixed price, and signs a one-step contract for delivery on a specified date. Such a market depends on having complete information about a need; having a standardized, off-the-shelf product; having a predictable budget; being certain about the number of items to be purchased; and lacking concern about the continuing or future viability of the losing firms. Major defense acquisitions lack these normal features.

In major defense acquisitions, the relationship between buyer and producer is almost completely different from that assumed in the economist's model of the perfect marketplace. For example, defense acquisitions have only one domestic buyer. Producers typically compete during the design stage as opposed to the production stage. Quality and schedule are often as important as price. Products procured for defense acquisitions often require innovations in design and the use of new technologies (often subject to change while the product is being developed). Concern about using existing production capacity efficiently—to avoid increasing overheads on other ongoing programs in a facility—and sustaining unique industrial sectors also factor into the buyers' decisionmaking process. Unless these differences are taken into account, too much may be expected from attempts to increase the use of competition in defense purchases.

The basic argument for competition in defense procurement is that it stimulates innovation during the design-rivalry phase and reduces the government's costs of purchasing goods and services during production and operational support. Nonetheless, in some cases, it may be less costly for the government to forgo direct competition and rely on an alternative strategy. A DoD program manager must examine the different ways that competition might be introduced in a particular program, subject to the unique objectives and environment of that program, and make a judgment on whether competition is likely to be beneficial. The special nature of the environment for competition in defense procurement has been discussed extensively in other RAND publications.[1] The reader who is unfamiliar with the topic should find such literature helpful in understanding why there are inherent difficulties in introducing effective price competition into defense acquisitions. It should also provide a

---

[1] See, for example, Birkler et al. (2001).

key to understanding the variety of competition-enhancing arrangements that have been developed for defense acquisitions.

Use of Competition in Phase IV of the DD(X) Program

The objectives of competition, and whether it is a productive strategy, differ from one program to another and vary from one stage of a program to another, depending on the particular objectives and constraints affecting the program. The DD(X) program has already completed nearly ten years of design rivalry and risk-reduction development activities. That history has yielded a well-developed system design concept and a substantial body of knowledge and expertise created in the firms selected to perform the work. Those actions inevitably constrain the opportunities for further competition in future phases of the program.

Phase IV, the next phase of the program, will include four different kinds of activity:

- detail design, wherein the earlier design activities will be extended and refined to the point where actual construction of the first system can begin;
- construction, test, and demonstration of the lead ship;
- construction, test, and demonstration of the second ship, to be produced in a shipyard different from where the lead ship was produced;
- serial production to be performed at both shipyards.

Several firms have been participating in Phase III and would presumably be prepared to compete for certain portions of Phase IV:

- NGSS/Ingalls and BIW. NGSS/Ingalls (formerly Ingalls Shipbuilding Inc.) was the lead shipyard on the Gold Team that won the design rivalry competition and continued in that role during Phase III. BIW is also participating in Phase III as a subcontractor to NGSS. Both shipyards would be potential competitors for the detail ship design and shipbuilding activity.

- Raytheon Systems and Lockheed Martin. Raytheon was the warfare system designer on the Gold Team, and, at the start of Phase III, Lockheed was added as a radar array supplier and system designer. Raytheon has been the lead source of technology development on the warfare system during Phase III, with Lockheed as subcontractor for some elements of the system. Both might be considered as potential competitors for supplying the warfare system during Phase IV.

- NGSS was the corporate owner of Ingalls Shipbuilding during the later phases of the design rivalry competition and is serving as design agent and overall contract manager during Phase III. The Navy prefers to retain the model of a single prime contract agent through the detail design task of Phase IV to ensure proper integration of all system components. However, a different model might be preferred for the serial production activity, as discussed in Chapter Four.

With that background of future DD(X) program tasks and plausible competitors to perform those tasks, it was necessary to examine the practicality and desirability of holding formal competitions for those tasks. We performed that analysis in two steps. We first created a simple matrix of options, showing each possible combination of competition and major task. We then assessed the likely benefits and penalties of each option, drawing from the background of information and understanding of competition in military acquisition programs discussed above. The remainder of this chapter will describe the results of that analysis.

A Matrix of Options for Competition in Phase IV

It would be technically possible to hold a competition at each step of Phase IV: compete the detail design of both the warfare system and the ship, compete production of the lead ship system, compete each of the serial production ships, and compete the task of system integration management throughout detail design and production. Only production of the second ship would be exempt from that process because we assume it would be allocated to the shipyard that did not produce the lead ship.

In this analysis, the task of system integration management was not examined as a candidate for competition, simply because there is no historical experience on which such an analysis could be based. The absence of system integration management in the following discussion of competition should not be construed as either favoring or rejecting the use of competition for that task.

The matrix of broad options examined in this study is depicted in Figure 2.1. We examined each option, considering first the principal objectives of such a competition (design rivalry or cost reduction?) and then drew from history to estimate whether the benefits are likely to exceed the costs.

Should Detail Design of the Warfare System Be Competed?

As noted earlier, the *design rivalry* for the warfare system occurred in Phases I and II of the DD(X) program, with the Gold Team,

Figure 2.1
Matrix of Competition Options for DD(X) Phase IV

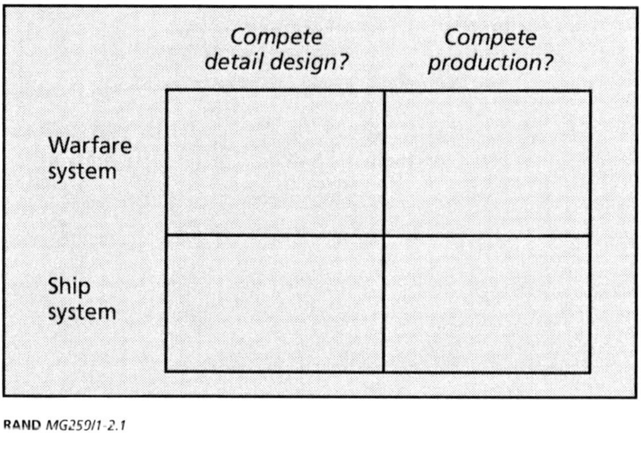

including Raytheon Systems, being selected as the winner in June 2002. That design, subsequently augmented by incorporating some elements contributed by Lockheed Martin, is being further refined during the three years of Phase III. By the end of Phase III, the team of Raytheon and Lockheed Martin, and their principal subcontractors, will have expended roughly $1.5 billion in development of the warfare system design. An important portion of that work will have been devoted to software, including three out of a planned seven software releases and an extensive facility for software testing.

If the warfare system were to be subject to a new competition at the beginning of Phase IV, the present team would have a very large advantage over any potential competitor. In a design rivalry, a competitor might have the apparent advantage of a clean start, using technologies introduced over the past three or four years, and thus be able to offer a design that promised better performance than the present Raytheon–Lockheed Martin design. However, such an approach would pose serious potential costs in time, dollars, and risks to the overall program. To reach a level of maturity and confidence in outcome comparable to the present design, any new design would almost certainly require several years and a substantial investment.

Considering the costs, risks, and program delays incurred in such a competition, we find no justification for a renewed *design rivalry* for the warfare system.

Similar arguments can be applied to the notion of holding a competition based on *cost of completing detail design* of the present system. Even if all work completed at the end of Phase III could be turned over to another firm, that firm would face a large task of assimilating the design details, training a staff, and establishing relationships with subcontractors and suppliers. The corresponding costs to the program in terms of delays and increased risks seem large compared with the possible savings resulting from a competition. Furthermore, we believe there would be enough uncertainty about the cost of detail design that a competitor would be unwilling to sign a firm fixed-price contract. Therefore, any savings based on bid prices resulting from a winner-take-all competition would be unenforceable estimates. On balance, we find no sound basis for holding a cost-based competition for completing detail design of the warfare system.

Finally, it should be noted that unlike the ship itself, the warfare system business (both design or production) entails no strong industrial-base reasons for distributing it among additional firms beyond those already participating. Similar electronic and digital systems are used in a wide variety of military systems and are produced by numerous firms. Industry health is not a critical issue here.

In summary, we find no justification for further competition for warfare system design. This is depicted in Figure 2.2.

Should Production of the Warfare System Be Competed?

Creating a second producer for the warfare system could be done at any time after the design had been stabilized and validated. There are at least two well-established procedures for introducing competition in the later phases of a production program:

- **Directed Licensing and Leader-Follower**—two arrangements whereby the government pays a developer-producer to transfer design data and production capability to a second contractor to make the same product; production is then either split, partially subcontracted to the follower, or competed.
- **Breakout**—the buyer acquires a subsystem directly from a subcontractor in either production or, in the case of spares, post-production.

Prior research, including a survey of results from production competition on 31 electronic systems or components, indicated that for systems and components similar to those covered in the survey, there is at least an even chance of recovering the investment in a second production line through competitively achieved price reductions.[2] However, the DD(X) warfare system is not characteristic of

---

[2] See Chapter Five of Birkler et al. (2001).

Figure 2.2
Competing Detail Design of DD(X) Warfare System Is Not
Attractive

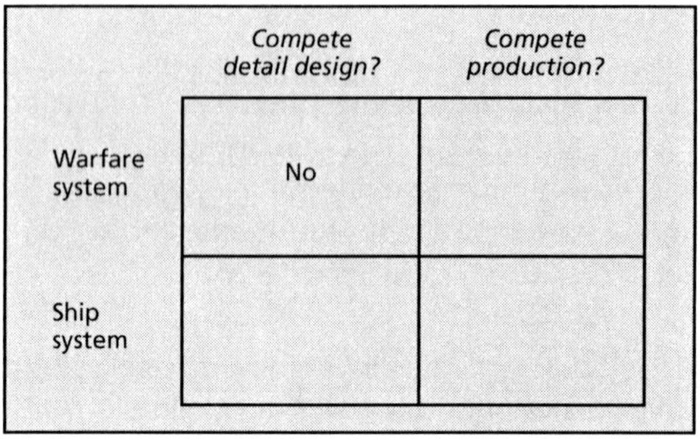

	Compete detail design?	Compete production?
Warfare system	No	
Ship system		

RAND MG259/1-2.2

the systems included in that survey of past experience. Two differences stand out. First, the DD(X) warfare system will likely have a relatively small production run of maybe two dozen units, and the design will probably not be stabilized until several have been produced and installed on the ships. Furthermore, the spiral development approach planned for the DD(X) means that major upgrades will occur in that short production run. Therefore, cost recovery for even the enduring system elements must occur in the course of 20 or fewer units, and over only a few units for the elements subject to upgrade. Those quantities are far less than typical of the competitive production data base. Second, many components of that system will be procured on a competitive basis from vendors, so only a portion of the final cost would be subject to competition at the prime level.

We judge that competition for DD(X) warfare system production is unlikely to recover the investment needed to set up a second production source. However, forgoing competition in the initial production of the warfare system does not necessarily prevent introduction of competition later if conditions warrant it.

Future contingencies cannot be foreseen now with sufficient clarity to judge the appropriateness of any particular strategy for application to the DD(X) program, but in the near term we can see little opportunity for using competition to yield reductions in warfare system production cost. Figure 2.3 shows our competition matrix with this assessment added.

Should Ship System Production Be Competed?

The design and production of a major ship is very different from that of a warfare system, and consideration of how competition can be employed in Phase IV of the DD(X) ship design and production demands a separate analysis. We first outlined an extensive menu of how competition could be employed in ship design and construction during Phase IV. However, certain sequences of competition seem impractical. For example, the process of detail design is tightly linked with lead ship construction because details of manufacturing tooling and procedures must be incorporated at every step of the detail design. Consequently, we did not consider the option of competing detail design, then competing lead ship construction, assuming instead that the winner of the detail design competition would also be awarded lead ship construction. Another situation where competition

Figure 2.3
Competing Production of DD(X) Warfare System Is Not Attractive

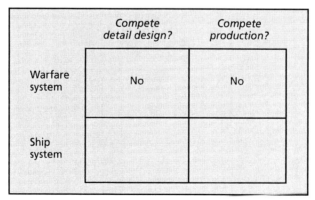

would be technically possible but impractical could occur if the Navy elects to have both shipyards team on the initial design task. It might be technically possible for the Navy to then hold a competition for lead ship construction, but the prospect of such competition would surely constrain the shipyards from fully cooperating on the joint detail design task.

After a subjective screening of impractical competition options, the remaining options are outlined in Figure 2.4.

In the DD(X) program, use of competition in production is strongly affected by four factors. First, the Navy has announced a policy to provide both shipyards with business types and amounts needed to ensure that both will remain and be available as strong competitors in future surface combatant ship programs. This policy effectively prevents awarding a low bidder with a predominant share of the shipbuilding business. We cannot predict with precision how much DD(X) production business will be required to keep each ship-

Figure 2.4
Possible Paths for DD(X) Ship Design and Production

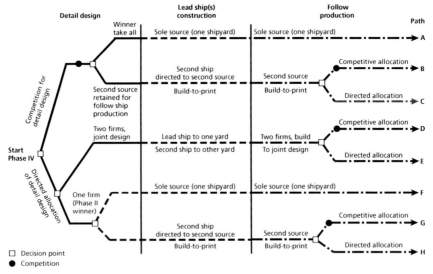

yard in business. The Navy plans to split production evenly between the two shipyards, and the analysis of labor demand described in the following chapter provides little basis for deviating from that policy.

A second, and related, factor is that production rates of the DD(X) are projected to be relatively low, averaging about two ships per year. Thus, annual contracts where less than half the work is allotted to one yard would yield very low construction activity at that yard, unless other ship construction programs were also available. Use of multiyear contracts would enable some uneven allocation of production in response to competitive cost bids, but Congress has been reluctant to fund multiyear shipbuilding contracts and that practice cannot be relied on.

A third factor arguing against competitive ship construction awards is that ship construction costs typically remain uncertain until each yard has constructed at least one ship. This is reflected by the cost growth in three cases of competitive awards for ship design and lead ship construction, as shown in Figure 2.5.[3] Furthermore, by the time the first two DD(X) ships are completed, nearly half of the remaining ships will have been placed under contract. Thus, true price competition will not be practical for at least the first half of the DD(X) ship production program.

Finally, we find little historical evidence supporting the expectation of reduced construction cost through competitive bidding. Such experience, outlined in Appendix B, shows that some programs appear to reflect competition-induced cost reductions but others do not. There are too few programs to examine, and too many differences among the programs, to permit any confident conclusions about the effects of competition on ship construction cost.

As in the case of warfare system production, we cannot foreclose the option for some form of competition during later stages of the program. However, we conclude that competition during the

_____

[3] See Figure A.6 in Appendix A and Figures B.2 and B.4 in Appendix B for description of data sources.

Figure 2.5
Cost Experience of Three Competitive Programs: CG 47, DDG 51, and LPD 17

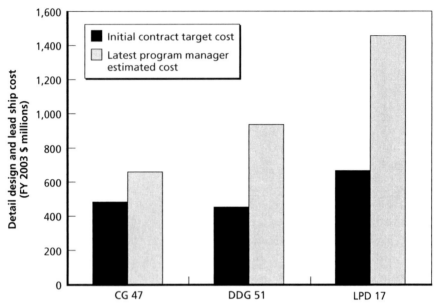

NOTE: CG 47, DDG 51, and LPD 17 were competitive awards for detail design and lead ship construction.
RAND *MG259/1-2.5*

initial production is not warranted. Figure 2.6 shows the matrix with this assessment added.

Should Ship System Detail Design Be Competed?

The final decision is whether to compete detail design of the ship. As in the case of the warfare system, there is no historical basis for anticipating a productive *design rivalry* in DD(X) ship design at this point. The design offered by the Gold Team won the design rivalry in June 2002, and that design has been extensively refined during the three years of Phase III. There is no reason to expect that a new design rivalry at this point would yield a design significantly better than the one existing at the end of Phase III, or one that offered a comparable level of maturity and remaining risks. It is always possible

Figure 2.6
Competing Production of Initial DD(X) Ship Systems Is Not Practical

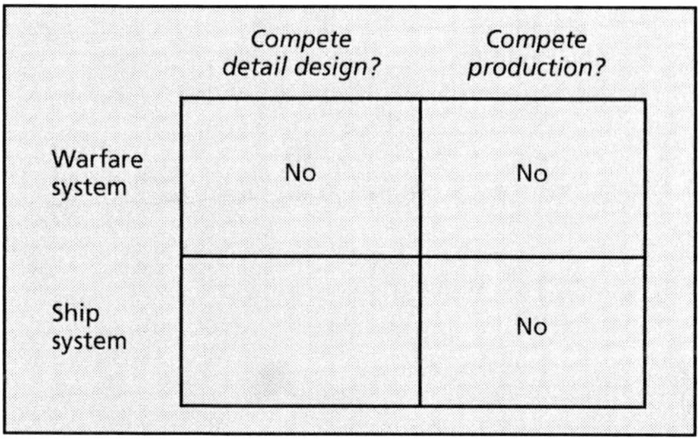

	Compete detail design?	Compete production?
Warfare system	No	No
Ship system		No

to offer a new design concept that, on paper, appears better than a design almost ready for production, but that would not be useful to the DD(X) program at this point.

Similarly, history offers no basis for expecting *cost benefits* from competing the detail design of the ship, as indicated by the data shown in Figure 2.5. The fact that the costs shown comprise both detail design and construction of the lead ship again reflects the difficulty of separating detail design from lead ship construction.

Introducing a competition for detail ship design at this stage of the program could also plausibly be expected to increase the overall program cost because of the delays that would be introduced. To conduct a competition would require a minimum of six months and perhaps up to a year if the source selection was contested. During that time it would be necessary for the warfare system producer to sustain their design staff and production facilities. We have not attempted to estimate the costs incurred, but they would be substantial. Additionally, the shipyards would suffer more turbulence in labor staff because of an extended transition from DDG 51 to DD(X) production.

In summary, we find no basis for expecting net benefits, in either design quality or cost of the design activity, from competing the detail design of the DD(X) ship system. Figure 2.7 shows the completed matrix with this assessment added.

If detail design is not competed, two options remain for how it should be managed: either as a joint effort engaging the design teams of both shipyards or having it performed in one shipyard with the second shipyard contracted to build to that design under a leader-follower arrangement. These are represented in Figure 2.8.

Here the distinction between alternatives is less clear-cut. A leader-follower approach with the leader directed to perform a sole-source detail design might reduce the initial cost of the task by eliminating all effort required to coordinate work of two firms. However, in such an arrangement the "follower" shipyard typically incurs some cost in reviewing the design presented to them, aligning specifications and production processes with their own practices, and generally ensuring that when produced in their shipyard the product will conform to specifications. Furthermore, a sole-source design would not be expected to make maximum use of the experience and expertise of both shipyard design teams, and that might be reflected in higher production costs throughout the serial production program.

Alternatively, a joint design effort might initially be projected to cost more that a directed sole-source effort because of coordination of personnel and methods, travel expenses, etc., but the result would likely benefit the overall program by combining the best features of both shipyard design staffs. It would have the strong added advantage of strengthening both industry design teams and thereby supporting the desire to sustain both shipyards for future competitions and for further design upgrades throughout the DD(X) production program. A critical element of this approach is the need to have true cooperation between the two shipyards. Whether this can be achieved through contract incentives is not apparent at this time.

On balance, we believe that a joint design program with both shipyards involved on an approximately equal basis would be the preferred approach, if it can be practically implemented. For that to work, it seems likely that both firms would have to be assured that

Figure 2.7
Competing Either Detail Design or Production of DD(X)
Ship System Is Not Attractive

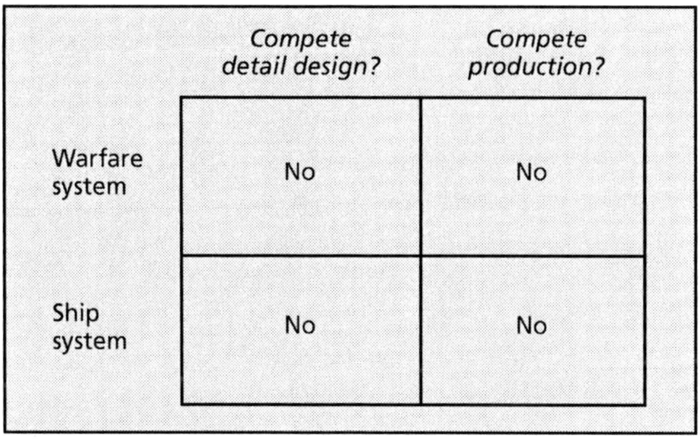

	Compete detail design?	Compete production?
Warfare system	No	No
Ship system	No	No

RAND MG259/1-2.7

Figure 2.8
Two Options for Managing Detail Design in the Absence of Competition

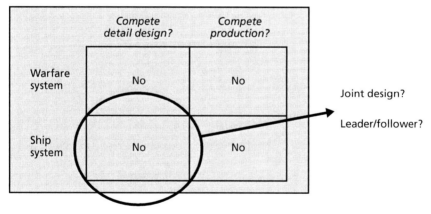

RAND MG259/1-2.8

they would not later be placed in the position of competing for serial production. Only with such assurances would each shipyard be reasonably expected to contribute their best staff and intellectual property to the joint design effort.

In summary, despite the classic arguments favoring competition in procurement actions, we believe that the special circumstances that currently exist in the DD(X) program provide persuasive reasons for joint design and allocated production, together with incentives for cost reduction.

CHAPTER THREE

Effects of the DD(X) Production Program on the Shipbuilding Industry

The U.S. Navy relies on industry to design and build its ships. Today only two shipyards are capable of supporting Navy needs for such ships as the DD(X), and during the next 15 to 20 years the DD(X) program is expected to represent the major portion of overall shipbuilding business for this general class of ships. It is widely believed that an industrial base consisting of two shipyards will serve the Navy better than a single firm, and it is the Navy's stated intention to ensure, to the extent practical, that both shipyards remain in business throughout the DD(X) program. However, implementing such a policy is likely to incur costs, and, as explained in the previous chapter, such costs might not be recovered through competitive pressures. It is therefore appropriate to examine the question of how the DD(X) ship construction program should be organized to provide the best outcomes in terms of supporting the shipbuilding industry while constraining DD(X) program shipbuilding costs.

Analysis Approach

The cost of building a basic ship platform (including hull and mechanical and electrical systems but excluding the warfare system supplied by other firms) depends in part on how the schedule of that particular ship construction meshes with other tasks at the shipyard. While the cost of purchased material will also depend somewhat on schedule, the cost of providing the ship construction labor in the

31

proper skills and experience levels can be very sensitive to the ship construction schedule and how that schedule meshes with other jobs at the shipyard. We believe labor costs are a good proxy for the overall cost consequences of different construction schedules and different patterns of allocation of ships among the shipyards.

We therefore explored this issue by estimating the shipyard labor demands and the cost of providing a labor force capable of meeting those demands for different DD(X) ship production allocations and schedules.

The primary tool used for this portion of the study is the N81 Shipbuilding Model developed by RAND in an earlier study sponsored by the Assessments Division of the Deputy Chief of Naval Operations for Resources, Warfare Requirements, and Assessment (OPNAV/N81). As described in the documentation (Arena, 2004), the tool consists of four linked models. The first model, the force transition model, determines when new ships are acquired and when existing ships retire, based either on a given acquisition plan or a desired force structure. The outputs from the force transition model serve as important inputs to the next two models: the industrial base model and the operations and support (O&S) cost model. The industrial base model calculates workforce demands and labor costs based on the acquisition plan. The O&S cost model determines the O&S costs for ships in the fleet. The last model, the financial adjustments and assumptions model, allocates the various funding streams to the appropriate budget categories, adjusts the base year of the costs to a fixed year, and applies a discount rate for discounted cash flow analysis. The tool architecture is depicted in Figure 3.1.

The industrial base module of the model was the primary tool used in this report. That module performs several functions, as outlined in Figure 3.2.

Given appropriate input data on the production schedule for each ship being built in the shipyard and labor demands for each ship type in terms of man-hours per calendar quarter by skill type, the model can determine the demands for direct labor for each quarter at each shipyard, in either full-time equivalents (FTE) or man-hours.

Figure 3.1
Shipbuilding Model Architecture

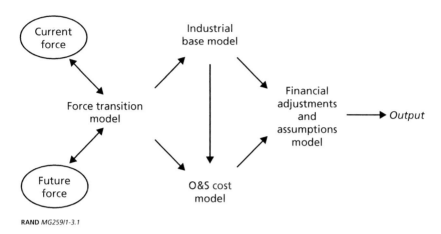

RAND *MG259/1-3.1*

Figure 3.2
Modeling Shipyard Labor Costs

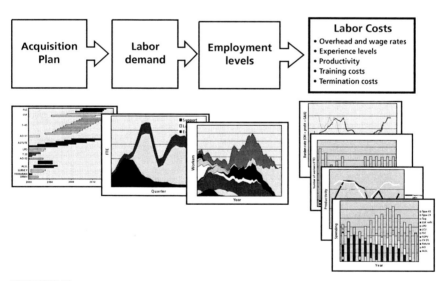

RAND *MG259/1-3.2*

To perform this analysis we obtained data from each shipyard on their estimates of the man-hours required to build a DD(X) by skill (e.g., electricians, shipfitters, etc.) and by calendar quarter, together with their wage and overhead rates necessary to estimate total cost of labor demand. We also obtained the shipyard estimates of labor required for construction of the other ships scheduled to be built in those shipyards. Other shipyard costs, such as purchased materials, are less sensitive to changes in overall workload and construction schedule. The data we collected are described in greater detail below and in Appendix C.

We will describe our analysis process using a fictitious shipyard to illustrate each step, then describe the results in general terms. Detailed quantitative results are reported in a companion document.[1]

The description of the analysis process starts with Figure 3.3 showing a plot of direct labor demand in FTE staff versus time for a fictitious shipyard, broken down by project. The top line of this figure shows a total labor demand of, for example, 6,000 FTEs in 2011.

Ideally, labor *supply* (employment levels) would exactly equal labor *demand* in every quarter and for each skill type. However, labor demand often fluctuates over time. We refer to this as *turbulence*. The shipyards are constrained in how rapidly they can increase or decrease their employment levels by the local availability of labor possessing the requisite skills and experience levels, by the costs to train new workers, and by the severance costs associated with laying off workers. Because of these constraints it is impractical for a shipyard to exactly match labor supply with labor demand at all times. Instead shipyards find it practical to allow their labor supply to be in excess of the labor demand during some periods. We refer to the difference in labor supply and labor demand as *excess labor capacity*. For example, Figure 3.4 shows a plot of direct labor demand and supply for a fictitious shipyard. As we can see from the figure, the labor supply tracks the upper envelope of the labor demand curve.

The model estimates the minimum cost of the labor supply each shipyard must provide to meet labor demand. The estimate is calcu-

---

[1] John Schank et al., *The Navy's New Destroyer: Competition and Acquisition Strategy Options for Phase IV of the DD(X) Program*, Santa Monica, Calif.: RAND Corporation, 2005.

Figure 3.3
Direct Labor Demand for a Fictitious Shipyard

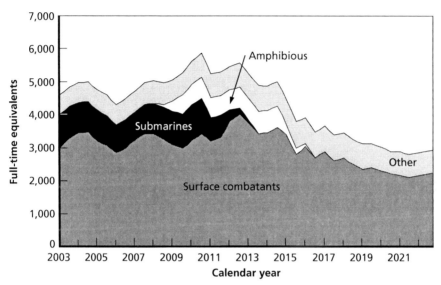

Figure 3.4
Labor Supply and Demand for a Fictitious Shipyard

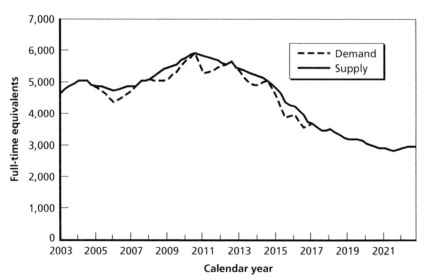

lated using a linear programming algorithm that minimizes the sum of direct labor costs and the indirect costs of hiring and training workers. It also calculates any loss of proficiency of new workers, compared to fully skilled workers, subject to the constraint that labor supply always meets demand and subject to constraints on the rate at which labor supply can fluctuate in the shipyard. The rate at which labor supply can fluctuate depends on many factors. For instance, it depends on attrition rates at the shipyard, the availability of workers by skill area and experience level, and shipyard policies on termination.

Once the model has estimated the required level of labor supply, it uses this information to estimate shipyard labor costs. The unburdened labor costs are calculated by multiplying labor supply in FTE per quarter by the quarterly wage rate. This is evaluated for each individual skill area and takes into account worker experience levels.

To estimate the burden rate, we asked each shipyard to provide an estimate of the 2003 manufacturing burden rate at their firm, and to supply us with volume sensitivity that indicates how the burden rate fluctuates with business volume. Our analytical model uses labor supply estimates as a measure of business volume and adjusts the estimate of burden rate according to the change in labor supply. The model uses this information to produce an estimate of burdened labor costs by calendar quarter. The costs are categorized by program (e.g., DD[X] or other ship type).

Sources of Input Data for the Model

We obtained the data necessary to drive the shipyard cost model from two sources: DD(X)-specific data were obtained from the DD(X) Program Office, and shipyard-specific data came directly from the two shipyards. These data are briefly summarized here.

DD(X) Descriptive Data

The DD(X) Program Office provided estimates of the total labor required to build each of 24 DD(X)ships, assuming that each shipyard would build 12. We estimated unit learning curves from the program office data by performing a least-squares fit to the data beginning with the second ship at each yard. We used the program office estimates for the first two ships at each yard and applied the learning curve to produce estimates for additional ships at each yard. The program office also provided a calendar schedule for ship production, up to an estimated 24 ships. That calendar schedule, described below in the summary of the base case, was used as a basis for all cases regardless of how we assumed the work to be distributed between the two shipyards.

Data Provided by the Shipyards

Shipyard data was requested from two firms: General Dynamics and NGSS.

General Dynamics owns several shipyards, including BIW, Electric Boat, and National Steel and Shipbuilding Company. BIW, the only General Dynamics shipyard that would be involved in DD(X) production, is located in Bath, Maine. Ship construction workers at BIW are unionized.

NGSS consists of three shipyards[2]:

- Ingalls: This full-service shipyard is in Pascagoula, Mississippi. Ship construction workers at Ingalls are unionized.
- Avondale: This full-service shipyard is in New Orleans, Louisiana. Ship construction workers at Avondale are not unionized.
- Gulfport: Currently, this is not a full-service shipyard. This yard formerly built panels for the other NGSS shipyards and is now developing a capability for composite shipbuilding. It is in Gulfport, Mississippi.

Ingalls is where most of the DD(X) production work allocated to NGSS will take place. However, Gulfport may be involved in the construction of the deckhouse. Also, NGSS can move work and

---

[2] Northrop Grumman also owns Newport News Shipbuilding, whose products include nuclear aircraft carriers and nuclear submarines.

workers between Avondale and Ingalls to handle peaks in demand, and this is done in practice.[3]

A questionnaire was sent to BIW and NGSS in August 2003 to gather information on the workforce and other (non-DD[X]) projects at the shipyards. The questionnaire is included as Appendix C. It gathered information including but not limited to:

- The number of direct workers employed at the shipyard over the past ten years, categorized by skill area (for example, electricians and machinists).
- The experience levels and associated productivity of the current workers and of typical new hires.
- Wage rates for direct workers by skill and experience level.
- Manufacturing burden rates for the current business base and volume sensitivity of burden rate to business base.
- Attrition rate, hiring availability, and limits on termination rates for direct workers, by skill and experience level.
- Training, hiring, and termination costs.
- Profiles of labor demand (in FTEs) for each project under way or planned for the shipyard. These profiles show the number of FTEs in each skill that are needed in each quarter of production to produce a single unit.
- Unit learning-curve slopes associated with each profile of labor demand.
- The current schedule for all activities under way or planned for the shipyard.

Currently, non-DD(X) work at BIW is largely devoted to construction of DDG 51–class ships. There is also a small demand for labor to support yard planning activities and some engineering support for design projects done in conjunction with other General Dynamics divisions, mainly Electric Boat. Non-DD(X) work at Ingalls consists of DDG 51–class ships, LHD, LHA(R) (Amphibious

---

[3] Workers have also been moved between Newport News and other NGSS shipyards.

Assault Ship Replacement), LPD 17–class ships, and NSC (National Security Cutter) work for the U.S. Coast Guard. Ingalls also provided data on projects they shared with Avondale shipyard, a sister division of NGSS. In all cases, this "other work" was aggregated and presumed to continue as scheduled regardless of the DD(X) production assigned to that shipyard.

Analysis Results: Base Case

We first created a "base case" that reflects the DD(X) program of record. This served as a reference point for all subsequent variations performed to explore the effects of different assumptions on work distributions and of possible delays in the start of ship production.

The program office provided the projected DD(X) production schedule shown in Table 3.1. This schedule distributes ships alternatively to each shipyard, with the lead ship going to Ingalls. Note, however, that the production schedule is not uniform over time.

Labor Demand

We first estimated the change in total labor demand over time, relative to the demand in 2003, at Ingalls and BIW, respectively, for the base case. A nearly 100 percent increase in labor demand at Ingalls occurs around 2021 during the early stages of the DD(X) program, with work on multiple ships under way as indicated by the schedule in Table 3.1. A decrease in the workforce at BIW occurs in the 2007 to 2011 time frame because of the gap between completion of the DDG 51–class work and the start of work on the second DD(X) ship.

Labor Supply

We used the shipyard labor model described above to determine the minimum-cost labor supply needed to satisfy labor demand, subject to constraints on the availability of workers by skill and experience level, attrition rates, and other factors. One important set of parame-

Table 3.1
Base Case DD(X) Production Schedule

Ship	Shipyard	Start Fabrication	Delivery Date
1	INGALLS	8/15/2007	8/15/2011
2	BIW	4/15/2008	4/15/2012
3	INGALLS	3/15/2009	4/15/2012
4	BIW	3/15/2010	4/15/2013
5	INGALLS	3/15/2010	4/15/2013
6	BIW	7/15/2010	7/15/2013
7	INGALLS	11/15/2010	11/15/2013
8	BIW	3/15/2011	3/15/2014
9	INGALLS	9/15/2011	9/15/2014
10	BIW	3/15/2012	3/15/2015
11	INGALLS	9/15/2012	9/15/2015
12	BIW	3/15/2013	3/15/2016
13	INGALLS	9/15/2013	9/15/2016
14	BIW	3/15/2014	3/15/2017
15	INGALLS	9/15/2014	9/15/2017
16	BIW	3/15/2015	3/15/2018
17	INGALLS	9/15/2015	9/15/2018
18	BIW	3/15/2016	3/15/2019
19	INGALLS	9/15/2016	9/15/2019
20	BIW	3/15/2017	3/15/2020
21	INGALLS	9/15/2017	9/15/2020
22	BIW	3/15/2018	3/15/2021
23	INGALLS	9/15/2018	9/15/2021
24	BIW	3/15/2019	3/15/2022

ters is the hiring rate—a measure of the availability of workers in the workforce market. A hiring rate of 10 percent for a particular skill means that the shipyard can increase the number of workers employed at the yard in that skill by 10 percent per year.

We refer to the hiring rates estimated from data provided by the shipyards as the *nominal hiring rates*. Those rates were higher than those used in other recent shipbuilding studies, so we decided to also estimate the shipyard labor supply using a more conservative estimate of hiring rates in order to provide a sensitivity analysis.[4] For this purpose, we assumed a hiring rate of about half the rate suggested by the shipyards. We shall refer to these as the *low hiring rates*. The parametric variation in hiring rates is important because a low hiring rate means that the shipyard must retain more excess labor to meet

---

[4] See Birkler et al. (1998).

demands when work expands, thus increasing costs. It seems likely that the actual hiring rates achieved by the shipyards over the next several years will fall between the two extremes shown here.

Labor Cost

Our cost analysis was performed using constant-dollar analysis, in keeping with the Office of Management and Budget (OMB) guidelines for cost-benefit analyses for the government (OMB, 1992). The estimated cost stream represents the annual cost of fully burdened direct labor for all programs at both Ingalls and BIW, assuming the nominal hiring rate, and represented in FY 2003 dollars. Note that we estimated cost, not price.

We then estimated the total fully burdened direct labor cost for all programs at both Ingalls and BIW by summing over the years 2003–2022. These totals include the labor cost for the other programs in each shipyard because those costs will be affected by changes in DD(X) schedule and allocation.

In the subsequent cases we examined, the only factor that is changed is the allocation or schedule of the DD(X) ships, so changes in cost stem solely from effects of variations in the DD(X) program.

Analysis Results: Alternative Cases

The base case described above shows that the program of record would result in some turbulence in labor levels at both shipyards. It also reflects a nominal plan to distribute the shipbuilding business evenly between the two shipyards. Other cases can easily be imagined, however, and we explored the likely effects of three kinds of variations on the base case:

- Would switching the lead ship construction to BIW produce less overall turbulence in required labor supply and thus to lower overall costs?
- What would be the effect of possible delays in starting the shipbuilding program?

- Would a change in the distribution of ships, leading to one shipyard producing more than half the total, be beneficial to either the program or the shipbuilding industry?

We examine these issues in the remainder of the chapter.

Lead Ship to BIW

Here we assume the same production schedule as that shown for the base case (Table 3.1), except that BIW produces the first ship, Ingalls produces the second ship, and the two shipyards continue to alternate production until all 24 ships are produced. All other assumptions are identical to the base case.

By comparison with the base case, the turbulence in labor demand between 2009 and 2013 is more severe if the first ship is given to BIW. It should be noted that NGSS owns the Avondale shipyard located near their Ingalls facility and has some ability to move work between yards. Our results do not take into account the possibility of NGSS moving work between these two yards.

By comparison with the labor demand for the base case, the labor demand at BIW does not fluctuate as rapidly under this plan.

Directing the lead ship to BIW instead of Ingalls results in a reduction of turbulence in labor demand at BIW at the expense of increased turbulence in labor demand at Ingalls. However, there is negligible difference in total labor cost if the lead ship is directed to BIW instead of Ingalls.

Alternative Case: One-Year Delay in Start of Ship Production

Next we evaluate the implications of a one-year delay in DD(X) ship production. We assume the same production schedule as that shown for the base case, except that we increase all dates in Table 3.1 by exactly one year. Additionally, we extend the DD(X) nonrecurring work by one year but keep the overall DD(X) nonrecurring man-hour estimate unchanged (there is no change in effort, only dura-tion). All other assumptions are identical to those of the base case.

Compared with the labor demand for the base case, the labor turbulence between 2009 and 2013 is more severe at both shipyards.

A one-year delay in schedule results in an increase of between 2 and 3 percent in total shipyard labor cost, depending on the assumed hiring rate

Alternative Case: One-Year Delay and Lead Ship at BIW

Next we evaluate the implications of combining a one-year delay of schedule with directing the lead ship to BIW. We assume the same production schedule as that shown for the base case, except that we introduce a one-year delay and direct the lead ship and all odd-number ships to BIW and second ship and all even-number ships to Ingalls. That is, we increase all dates in Table 3.1 by exactly one year and reverse the order of the shipyards. Additionally, we extend the DD(X) nonrecurring work by one year but keep the overall DD(X) nonrecurring man-hour estimate unchanged (there is no change in effort, only in duration). All other assumptions are identical to the base case, including production man-hour estimates and non-DD(X)-related work.

A one-year delay causes an increase in turbulence in labor demand at both yards between 2009 and 2013.

A one-year delay in schedule and directing the lead ship to BIW results in a labor cost premium of between 2 and 3 percent in total shipyard labor costs, depending on the assumed hiring rate. This is the same result we found for the one-year-delay case with the lead ship directed to Ingalls. In summary, there is little impact of directing the lead ship to one shipyard versus the other, even with the combined effects of a one-year delay of schedule.

Alternative Workload Cases

Our base case involves a 50-50 split in DD(X) production: 50 percent (12 hulls) are produced by Ingalls and 50 percent (12 hulls) are produced by BIW. We next explore different DD(X) workload cases. We developed estimates of the shipyard labor costs for each case. We do not attempt to estimate whether each shipyard will remain in business for each case. To do so would require estimating the behavior of the decisionmakers involved, and we lack a method for such an evaluation. However, we will quantify the labor demands at each shipyard in the near and far term. This information would likely have an important role in the decision by each firm to remain in business or not. We note that another important input for the decisionmaker would be profit, which requires an estimate of price. We only provide estimates of labor cost, not price and not profit.

We used our analytical models to estimate labor demand, labor supply, and burdened direct labor cost associated with four alternative workload cases:

- 67 percent (16 DD[X] ships) to Ingalls, 33 percent (8 DD[X] ships) to BIW.
- 67 percent (16 DD[X] ships) to BIW, 33 percent (8 DD[X] ships) to Ingalls.
- 100 percent (24 DD[X] ships) to Ingalls.
- 100 percent (24 DD[X] ships) to BIW.

In these calculations we assume the same start fabrication and delivery dates as those shown in Table 3.1. The lead ship is directed to Ingalls in all cases except when 100 percent is directed to BIW. Construction alternates between yards until at least one yard has produced its full share.

The results show that the base case does not minimize or maximize fully burdened labor costs. However, such estimates ignore the implications of a firm going out of business, which is increasingly likely with a nonequitable workload allocation. It also ignores any effects of changes in competitive environment.

Summary Observations

Implications of Different Production Schedules

We found that a one-year delay in DD(X) production schedule exacerbates turbulence in labor demand. The labor demand could be met, provided we allow for sufficient excess labor capacity to meet labor demands. The cost implications are a premium of between 2 percent and 3 percent in fully burdened direct labor costs or all programs at both shipyards during the 2003–2022 time period. This is approximately the fully burdened direct labor cost of an additional DD(X).

Directing the lead ship to one shipyard or the other has a negligible impact on labor costs. This result holds even in the case of a one-year delay in schedule.

Effects of Alternative Workload Allocations

We cannot predict the minimum amount of work required by each firm to remain in business.

The base-case workload allocation does not minimize or maximize total shipyard labor costs to the program. However, it obviously gives an equitable share of DD(X) production to the two yards, which may be a reasonable solution in absence of information on what each yard will require to remain in business.

CHAPTER FOUR

DD(X) Phase IV Contracting Issues and Options

Phase III of the DD(X) program included several tasks focused on developing and demonstrating new technologies and designs that could be incorporated into the overall DD(X) system. Supported by RDT&E funds, the tasking also included the responsibility to ensure that the various components and technologies being developed could be incorporated into an overall system. Partly because of the technical challenge posed by the overall integration effort and the required coordination of activities at two shipyards, two major developers of integrated electronic systems, and several smaller firms, the Navy chose to place the entire Phase III activity under one contract, awarded to NGSS, with BIW and Raytheon serving as subcontractors to NGSS, and Lockheed as a subcontractor to Raytheon.

Phase IV of the program presents a somewhat different set of objectives and taskings. The initial task, also supported by Research, Development, Test, and Engineering (RDT&E) funds, will consist of completing detail design of the overall system, including production design of all system elements. That will be followed by construction, test, and demonstration of the lead ship (also RDT&E-funded), construction of the second ship at the alternative shipyard (now planned for shipbuilding and conversion, Navy [SCN], funding), and then serial construction of up to 24 ships, all SCN-funded. If the serial production program proceeds as planned, further technology development and system upgrades are envisioned under the spiral-development management concept.

In addition to the conventional objectives of designing and producing a system, the Navy had two additional objectives stemming from the policy decision to ensure that each shipyard received enough business to remain a viable participant and competitor in future projects:

- Sustain the surface combatant shipbuilding industrial base.
  - — Ensure that each shipyard has adequate design and production work to enable participation in upgrades, CG(X), and other future programs.
- Achieve efficiencies in DD(X) through interfirm cooperation.
  - — Joint design and integration of full system.
  - — Joint purchase of common parts and material.
  - — Joint management of test and acceptance procedures.

Looking ahead to that evolving set of tasks, it is not obvious that the contracting strategy used in Phase III is appropriate for Phase IV. The third task in the present study was to explore different possible contracting strategies and to develop some understanding of the expected advantages and disadvantages of each. We did that by first describing in generic form the main options, then summarizing how each could be applied to the different steps of Phase IV.

Another factor that affects a contracting strategy is that, as the program moves through different phases, the combination of commercial entities changes. During detail design, the activities of all three entities (warfare system provider, plus each shipyard) must be integrated by some overall management process. During construction of each ship, operations of that shipyard must be integrated with production of the warfare system. Finally, opportunities arise for cost reduction by continual joint procurement of material common to both shipyards. That is illustrated in Figure 4.1. Each combination poses different challenges to the contracting process.

Figure 4.1
Different Tasks Involve Different Sets of Contractors

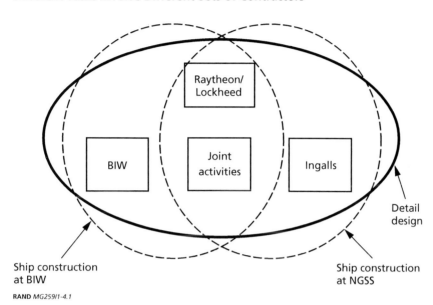

Model 1: Separate Contracts to Each Major Participant

A conventional contracting strategy, one that has been used on most major Navy ships in the recent decades, is illustrated in Figure 4.2. Here the Navy contracts separately with each major firm involved in the program, and the Navy Project Office functions as the master system integrator.

   If applied to the first task of Phase IV, detail design of the total integrated system, this model would impose high demands on the Navy for technical integration management. The overall design resulting from these efforts would be a Navy product, and, contractually, the Navy would assume all risks for errors. Given recent trends in Navy staffing, such demands seem imprudent and unnecessary. Presumably the Navy could contract with a "third party" to perform such technical integration management, but that would require a

Figure 4.2
Contracting Model 1: Navy Contracts with Each Prime

Detail system design and system production

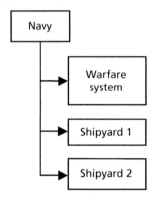

NOTE: During detail design, Navy manages total integrated design. During production, Navy supplies warfare system as GFE to shipyards, with shipyard responsible for final integration, test, and delivery.
RAND MG259/1-4.2

large investment of time (to select and award a contract) and effort to bring such a firm up to date on the critical technical issues involved in the DD(X) system design and on the inevitable risks associated with such a process. The new firm would be an outsider and find it difficult to understand the processes and personalities. This approach appears unattractive.

Given that detail design of the integrated system had been accomplished, this model could reasonably be applied to the following tasks of ship construction. The technical management burden imposed on the Navy would be greater than that performed under current contracts for the DDG 51–class destroyers because of the technical complexity and the unprecedented insertion of new revolutionary technologies. An example of this complexity is the integration of electronic emitters and the ship signature control methods. This is one of the more obvious reasons for the need for close coordination of all technical disciplines during detail design. In addition, this model would not then enable economies through joint procurement of equipment and material needed by both shipyards (unless the

Navy program office performed that task, which to our knowledge is unprecedented), and similarly it would be difficult to centralize final system test, check-out, and acceptance testing. For the Navy to buy all equipment and material needed by both shipyards would be time-consuming and risky. The Navy would have to use lists of equipment and material developed and provided by the shipyards, acquire the items, inspect them, and have them shipped to the shipyards in the time required by them. Failure in any part of this process would leave the Navy liable for damages incurred by the shipyards.

On balance, direct and traditional application of this model does not seem fully responsive to Navy needs in Phase IV.

Model 2: Single Contract with One Commercial Entity

This model is the conceptual opposite of Model 1. Here, the Navy identifies one firm, consortium, or other commercial entity to take contractual responsibility for managing all aspects of Phase IV.

Two possible variations of this strategy are shown in Figures 4.3 and 4.4. In one variation, a single firm acts as a full-service prime (FSP), managing all the firms engaged in the program and assuming full technical and contractual responsibility for the system.[1] This firm will receive the largest share of rewards (in terms of fee) and risks (of failures and liabilities). This concept is shown in Figure 4.3. The FSP could be one of the shipyards or the warfare system supplier or the parent company of any of the firms involved, such as NGSS (owner of Ingalls shipyard).

Another variation is shown in Figure 4.4. Here it is assumed that all, or most, of the major firms engaged in the program have

---

[1] This is the contracting approach typically used by the United Kingdom's Ministry of Defence for shipbuilding programs. For example, for their Type 45 program, BAE SYSTEMS is the full-service prime who subcontracts to Vosper Thornycroft and BAE SYSTEMS Marine for the construction of the platforms. This approach is also used for the U.S. Navy's *Virginia*-class production with Electric Boat acting as the full-service prime with a subcontract to Northrop Grumman Newport News.

Figure 4.3
Contracting Model 2A: Navy Contracts with a Full-Service Prime

Detail system design and system production

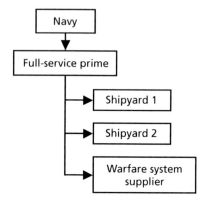

NOTE: Full-Service Prime might be any of the subcontractors shown or an independent system manager.
RAND *MG259/1-4.3*

joined forces and created a new legal entity in the form of a consortium or joint venture.[2] From the perspective of the Navy, not many distinctions exist between these two variations, because in each version the Navy would be interfacing with one entity that would have the full management, technical, and contractual responsibility for delivery of the ship system. Furthermore, either variation could be used for the detail design task at the beginning of Phase IV and the subsequent production of the ships and associated warfare systems.

A major advantage of such an arrangement is that it focuses all technical and management responsibilities in industry, thus relieving the Navy of that task. It would allow the Navy to interface directly with various members of the consortium because the Navy would have a direct contractual relationship with those members (instead of interfacing through the FSP). Furthermore, with the same organiza-

---

[2] This contract approach is used for the Coast Guard's Deepwater program where NGSS and Lockheed, two of the major contractors involved in the DD(X), formed a legal entity called Integrated Coast Guard Systems (ICGS). The Deepwater contracts are with ICGS.

Figure 4.4
Contracting Model 2B: Navy Contracts with Industry Consortium

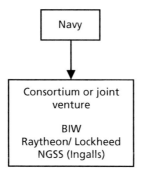

Detail system design and system production

NOTE: Separate contracts could be used for detail design, lead ship construction, second ship construction, etc., but basic contracting structure would remain constant.
RAND *MG259/1-4.4*

tion having responsibility for successive stages of the program, learning should be maximized and clear lines of contractual responsibility are established. Another possible advantage is that it would simplify the goal of centralizing joint procurement of common material, centralized management of checkout, acceptance testing of production units, etc.

However, challenges remain in implementing such an approach. The preferred approach is for a joint design, presuming full cooperation among the participants can be achieved. We anticipate a prolonged negotiation phase to reach an agreement that the Navy considered practical and that all firms to the consortium would sign up for. It seems plausible that asking the participating firms to design such a consortium working agreement would be more practical than having the Navy to attempt to outline such an agreement.

Given such an interfirm working agreement, the Navy could provide incentives using traditional contracting tactics. We suggest a few contracting strategies that might be effective:

- Detail design should be accomplished under a cost plus fixed-fee contract, with the fee split among the participants to be designated in the contract.
- The Navy should specify a target for funds distribution among the participants but allow some variation to accommodate uncertainties and risks involved in the design of such a complex system.
- Milestones for determining the stage of design completion should be specified, with ship construction allowed to begin at a specified milestone. This would provide schedule incentives.
- A joint management structure should be defined that meets Navy approval.
- An award-fee incentive should focus on Navy perceptions of each firm's willingness to engage in true joint efforts.

Any attempt to compete the subsequent ship production would almost certainly inhibit such cooperation.

These contracting strategies are also applicable for Model 3.

Model 3: A Blend of Strategies

We noted earlier that Phase IV of the DD(X) program involves several kinds of activities, some nonrecurring and some recurring. Therefore, it might be advantageous to consider a mix of contracting strategies with different kinds of contracts applied to different activities. On the surface, there appear to be no strong arguments against a sequence of different contracts, each tailored to individual tasks.

Figure 4.5 illustrates one such arrangement. Recall that the span of involvement of the various firms in the different activities, which we depicted in Figure 4.1, will affect the applicability of a contract form to a particular task. There appear to be strong arguments for having a single firm responsible for managing the technical integration of the disparate elements of the DD(X) weapon system during detail design. All of the firms involved in Phase III of the program

Figure 4.5
Contracting Model 3: Navy Employs a Blend of Single-Contract and Multicontract Models

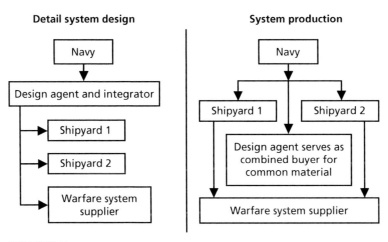

will likely participate in that detail design activity, suggesting that the detail design phase might be considered a logical extension of Phase III rather than having a new single firm control the entire design. That suggests a contract of Model 2 style for those nonrecurring tasks in Phase IV, such as detailed ship system and other key subsystem design, as well as spiral development activities. This contract would run concurrently with the ship production contracts and provide design updates as they occur. It would also be responsible for the centralized buying of common equipment and materials for efficiency. Whether that "prime" is a single firm or a consortium of the firms engaged in the DD(X) program appears to be mostly a matter of preference of the various participants as long as the Navy can interface with each of the critical participants in their area of expertise— i.e., Lockheed and its radar.

This model assumes that the contracts for production of ship systems will be to each shipyard, placing the shipyard in the role of single agent responsible for constructing, testing, and delivering the entire integrated DD(X) system produced by that shipyard. This portion of the model would be the traditional way of procuring ships.

Thus a contract similar to Model 1 would be indicated. It permits separate but equal contracts with the two shipyards where the Navy can ensure the industrial base is protected. The Navy can negotiate terms and conditions that match circumstances at each shipyard in an effort to achieve one of the DD(X)'s goals—timely and cost efficient ships.

One concern with this (and the first) model is the separation of the design and production activities in this phase of DD(X) program and the potential impact on contractual responsibilities. To execute Models 1 and 3, the government must take the outputs from the design efforts and use them as the input for negotiations and awards of the two shipbuilding contracts. With the acceptance of the design product, the government takes title. If something is lacking in the design that impacts production costs and schedule, the Navy may be required to equitably adjust the applicable contract, relieving the contractor of any responsibility, even though they might have been the developer of the design. The Navy should attempt to negotiate warranties on delivered designs that could mitigate the Navy's liability for faulty designs produced by the shipyards.

This situation of potential faulty (inadequate) designs is not an issue in Model 2 because the Navy never accepts the design products as finished items and uses them as government-furnished information (GFI) for the foundation of negotiations leading to a contract and thus the Navy is not liable for erroneous designs.

Summary Observations

The DD(X) is a technically complex, highly integrated weapon system that incorporates many technologies new to the shipbuilding industry. The successful integration of those technologies will present new and demanding management and integration challenges. We believe that industry is better prepared than the Navy to supply the necessary technical breadth and depth of such management skills. This position argues for industry to assume a greater role in technical integration management responsibilities than has been traditional in many shipbuilding programs. The Navy has acknowledged that trend by announcing a desire to minimize use of GFE and GFI in the DD(X) program. Because of this desire, Model 1 is not a suitable contractual strategy.

Models 2 and 3 are acceptable approaches. Because no effective competitive pressures exist now or in the near future, both models require the Navy to negotiate contractual incentives to encourage the correct behaviors by industry, even at the subcontractor levels.

CHAPTER FIVE

Conclusions

This report has examined a range of issues facing the DD(X) program as it nears the start of Phase IV, the stage that involves detail design of system components and production of lead units. The study addressed a number of acquisition and contracting issues and sought strategies that would help the Navy utilize competition in the most appropriate manner, employ existing production capacity efficiently, sustain America's core surface warship industrial base, and achieve program cost and schedule objectives.

The DD(X) program shares some characteristics inherent in many modern defense acquisition programs: high technological complexity and a limited opportunity to employ competitive sourcing in the later phases where detail design and production costs frequently argue against multiple suppliers. The program is further complicated by a mandate to support both Ingalls and BIW (the two remaining shipyards capable of developing and producing this class of ship) and by the fact that a third firm, Raytheon Systems (the developer/producer of the warfare system), adds as much value to the system as the ship producer.

Thus, the program does not involve a traditional single prime that manages many subcontractors and suppliers. Rather, it involves a team of two shipyards and a warfare system supplier, all of whose elements must be effectively integrated. This combination leads to complex issues on how to structure and manage the program.

As detailed below, the study led to three sets of conclusions regarding the choice of options for organizing and managing this next phase.

Conclusion One: Neither design rivalry for system configuration nor price competition for production of ship systems and warfare systems appears practical during the initial portions of Phase IV.

In major defense acquisition programs, competition is generally employed to achieve either or both of two objectives: selection of the best design concept, which results from a design rivalry that is held early in the program to select the best design concept, and control of costs, which results from a production price competition that is sometimes held later in the production phase. In the DD(X) program the design rivalry was held in the 1998–2002 time period and a team led by NGSS was declared winner. We find no precedent or any logical basis for reopening that issue in future phases of the program.

Price competition has been generally difficult to achieve in production of major weapon systems. Quantities are relatively small, and costs of starting and sustaining a second producer are relatively large, making such competition impractical in most cases. Some evidence of successful price competition in production of such ships as the DD(X) can be found, but achievement of similar results in DD(X) production would be severely limited by the Navy's stated policy of sustaining both shipyards as viable business entities and by the desire for cooperation between the shipyards during detail design. On balance, we conclude that price competition for ship production is impractical. Similarly, price competition for warfare system production will be impractical during at least the initial production because of the likely evolution of the design and very short production runs for any particular configuration.

Conclusion Two: The currently projected schedule of detail ship design and construction, together with the plan to distribute business equally to both shipyards, should provide enough business to sustain both shipyards as viable competitors for future surface combatant programs.

Only two shipyards in this country have a proven and current capability to develop and produce such combat ships as the DD(X). The Navy has announced a policy to sustain both shipyards so that they can contribute to future programs. The DD(X) program has three major mechanisms for providing such support to the shipyards: the rate at which the ships are built, the timing of the start of production at each shipyard, and the allocation of ships between the two shipyards. In this study, we used the production schedule (rate) proposed by the program office and did not perform a systematic examination of the effects caused by different production schedules. We did examine the effects on each of the two shipyards, and on the overall program costs, of varying the distribution of ships between the shipyards and of suffering a delay in the scheduled start of ship production.

Our analysis was based on estimates of the labor required to build the ships and of the costs of ensuring a supply of labor needed to meet that demand. We did not attempt to estimate management decisions on whether a particular production program was necessary to justify staying in the business of building such ships for the Navy.

We find that sustaining the present schedule for starting production of the first and subsequent DD(X) ships is important. Under the acquisition plan we examined, production of the first DD(X) was scheduled to start in August 2007—already too late to permit a smooth transition from other work to DD(X) production at both shipyards, with some resulting turbulence in demand for shipyard labor. Any additional delay would cause further turbulence and consequent cost of discharging, hiring, and training workers. We estimate that a one-year delay in start of production on the first ship (to about August 2008) would be manageable by both shipyards but would incur additional costs of between 2 and 3 percent in total shipbuilding costs. Delays of much more than a year would cause large disruptions in staffing at both shipyards and especially large at BIW—enough to jeopardize their continued existence.

The DD(X) Program Office postulated an even distribution of ships to the two shipyards, with the lead ship going to Ingalls, the second ship to BIW, and then alternating allocation of ships until the end of the production run. We estimated that shifting the allocation to as much as 67 percent to one shipyard or the other would be near the limit of practicality in terms of sustaining both shipyards as viable commercial concerns. Within that range, each shift might smooth the labor demand in one shipyard but make it worse in the other. No distribution uniformly stood out as the best alternative.

Conclusion Three: The presence of three major producers in the program, and the presence of both design and production tasks to be performed in Phase IV, suggests a mix of contracting strategies.

In most major weapon acquisition programs, the winner of the design rivalry becomes the single prime contractor for the remainder of the program, managing both the final development and the subsequent production. That policy was applied to Phase III of the DD(X) program, with NGSS designated as the system design agent responsible for integrating and managing the full range of design and risk-reduction activities performed by a number of firms serving as subcontractors. That practice could be extended into Phase IV. However, several aspects of the DD(X) program justify a reexamination of contracting methods for detail design and production.

One unique feature of the DD(X) program is that the warfare system represents roughly half the value of the total procurement actions in Phase IV. Should that much of the value be handled as a subcontract to the prime?

Another special feature is that the ship production will be allocated between two shipyards. Should one of those shipyards, or their parent corporation, be placed in the role of managing the other?

A third feature is that Phase IV comprises two very different kinds of activities: the final, detail design of the major components and of the complete, integrated system and the serial production of that system. It seems plausible that those two different activities should be managed under different contract structures.

We examined several different contracting methods that could be applied to Phase IV. One option was for the Navy to individually contract with each major member of the industry team now involved with the DD(X): each shipyard and the warfare system producer.

That would require the Navy to manage the total system integration during detail design and then to provide the warfare system as GFE to each shipyard during production. We deemed that to be a level of Navy involvement inconsistent with recent trends in Navy management staffing and with Navy policy.

A second group of options called for a single industry agent to contract with the Navy for full management of detail design and subsequent production. That single agent could be one of the firms now developing the DD(X) or a consortium of the several major participants. Such a model would be consistent with common practice, but the inherent competitive posture between the two shipyards could pose problems in the administration of such a process. A preferred strategy would be to encourage the key firms to create a consortium, with appropriate interfirm agreements and protocols worked out in advance to the greatest extent possible. The current agreement between Newport News Shipyard and Electric Boat for production of the *Virginia*-class submarine appears to be a useful model.

A third option was to use different contracting models for different tasks and phases of the project. Use of a single prime to manage detail design and final system integration has the powerful advantage of focusing authority and responsibility in a single agent. Also, the Navy could better control the production process by contracting directly with the shipyards, thus retaining an opportunity to inject some level of competition into the later stages of that production. Conversely, the separation of design from production introduces potential problems, and the contract for design and system integration would require very careful application of incentives to ensure adequate consideration of production processes at each shipyard. Such a multistage contracting strategy does not have a well-developed history or proven set of practices and must be approached with care.

CHAPTER SIX

Epilogue: July 2005

In the year since this research was conducted, many decisions were made affecting the program. As the program approached its scheduled Milestone B in April 2005 and its transition from Phase III (systems design) to Phase IV (detailed design and lead ship construction), changes were made to the expected number of DD(X)-class ships that would be procured, the build profile of those ships, and the government and industry organizational structures managing the program. These changes have affected the way the program can use competition in the future. This epilogue, written a year after the research was complete, discusses these changes to the program and their implications for competition in the future. The events occurred roughly between December 2004 and July 2005.[1]

The Plan Approaching Milestone B[2]

During Phase III, the DD(X) acquisition strategy included a high degree of centralization in program management. The Navy program office within Program Executive Office, Ships, PMS500, was the single government management agency for the program. While other Navy organizations provided important support, the PMS500 pro-

---

[1] Many important elements of the program—such as work on the EDMs—were unaffected by the changes in top-level acquisition strategy.

[2] The section is based largely on information in the Acquisition Strategy Report (ASR), approved by OSD on February 24, 2004.

gram manager was responsible for all elements of the DD(X) system, including both ship systems and combat systems.

A single contract had been awarded to a design agent (NGSS) at the beginning of Phase III. The design agent was responsible for administering the contract and allocating work between the two ship-yards and the mission equipment designer and integrator. Other contracts with system developers were with the design agent, not the Navy. The design agent was responsible for the critical system integration function, including both ship systems and weapon systems. The design agent established workshare and subcontract agreements, resolved intellectual property rights issues, and established technical and programmatic communications among government and industry participants.

This same government and industry structure was to be used in Phase IV. The design agent management structure was intended to facilitate total ship engineering and integration while preserving two viable shipyards to participate in ship construction. The Navy expected to award a single-source, cost-plus-award-fee contract to the design agent for Phase IV. The lead ship would be constructed at NGSS, with the second ship awarded to BIW. Subsequent ships would be allocated equally between the two shipyards, using cost-plus-incentive-fee contracts. Other contracts for weapon system development (advanced gun system, radar, peripheral launch vehicle systems, etc.) were to be administered by NGSS as the design agent.

The approved Phase IV plan included producing the first six ships. RDT&E funds were to be used for construction of the first ship, beginning in FY 2005. This represented a major departure from how lead ships had been funded in the past. The Navy argued that the flexibility inherent in the use of RDT&E funds was needed to meet the technical and integration challenges of DD(X).

The competition strategy for ship seven and beyond was to be proposed at Milestone B, scheduled for April 29, 2005. The Navy believed that this plan preserved an option for competition for ships seven and beyond, as well as at the lower tiers.

The Forcing Function—Number of Ships to Be Procured

The approved acquisition strategy, including the maintenance of two viable shipyards through the allocation of at least the first six ships, was based on an assumed total of 24–32 ships in the DD(X) class and a production rate of two to three ships a year (Goddard, 2005). The approved plan included lead ship award in FY 2005, followed by the allocated awards of two ships each in FY 2007 and FY 2008, and three ships in FY 2009, for a total of eight over the period FY 2005–FY 2009. Combined with the relatively large total buy, this appeared sufficient to maintain both shipyards at an acceptable cost per ship.

However, those assumptions changed during the process of developing the budgets for FY 2005 and FY 2006. The FY 2005 budget approved by Congress moved lead ship funding from RDT&E to SCN and slipped the lead ship to FY 2007 (DoD, 2005, slide 7). The Navy then had to reduce the build profile to make "fiscal" room in the SCN account. As part of the development of the FY 2006 budget that the President submitted to Congress in February 2005, Program Budget Decision (PBD) 753, issued in December 2004, reduced the total buy over the period by two ships, one each in FY 2009 and FY 2010, and reduced the build profile to one ship per year (OSD, 2004).

Table 6.1 summarizes the changes from the FY 2004 approved plan to the FY 2006 budget proposal. The Navy was forced to reduce the size of the total ship class to 8 to 12 ships and to make associated changes in the ship-build profile. As a result, shortly before Milestone

Table 6.1
Summary of Recent Changes to DD(X) Acquisition Strategy

	Total Build Quantity	Production Rate	Quantity FY 2004–FY 2011
Original Approved Acquisition Plan	24–32	2–3	8
FY 2006 Revised Acquisition Plan	8–12	1	5

NOTE: Data from DoD, 2005, slide 5.

B the Navy restructured the DD(X) acquisition strategy, including both the approach to contracting and competition.

The program office performed a series of analyses examining alternatives to the approved plan of single-source lead ship design and construction, with follow production to be equally split between the two shipyards. The analyses examined cost, schedule, and workload at the two shipyards for different allocation and competition scenarios (DoD, 2005, slides 2 and 6). The Navy determined that maintaining production at both shipyards was costly at the lower build rate.

A New Strategy

The Navy proposed a revised acquisition strategy designed to meet the challenges introduced by the changes to total quantity, production rate, and funding. That strategy envisioned a winner-take-all competition resulting in a single contract award to one shipyard that would act as the prime contractor for the program. The contract would include detailed design, systems integration, and completion of software development. There would be directed subcontracts to the combat systems integration and software development teams (DoD, 2005, slide 8). Program continuity would be maintained by awarding advanced procurement contracts to both shipyards and allocating some advanced procurement to key system developers for continuation of their efforts and transition to production in support of lead ship construction.

The competition would delay the start of lead ship fabrication by 12 months from the earlier plan's start date. The competitive strategy was estimated to save as much as $3.2 billion (then-year dollars) for a 10-ship buy over the period FY 2007–FY 2016. Estimated savings were derived from an improved learning curve at a single shipyard, and by limiting nonrecurring engineering investment to that shipyard.

OSD reviewed the revised strategy during March and early April 2005. On April 20, 2005, the Under Secretary of Defense for Acquisition, Technology, and Logistics (USD[AT&L]) issued an Acquisition Decision Memorandum authorizing the Navy to separate the combat systems and software development contracts from the lead ship detailed design and construction contract and issue a draft solicitation to obtain comments from industry on the proposed competitive strategy (USD[AT&L], 2005). However, USD(AT&L) did not approve the competitive strategy, stating that it was "premature to change the shipbuilder portion of the acquisition strategy." Milestone B, and approval for entry into Phase IV, was postponed, pending resolution of this issue.

The Navy briefed industry on the proposed changes to the program and released a draft solicitation in May 2005. A not-to-exceed $3 billion contract was awarded to Raytheon in late May to continue development of the combat systems for DD(X) (Weisman, 2005). Under this contract, Raytheon is developing five systems for DD(X):

- radar;
- sonar;
- ship's computing environment;
- external communications network; and
- advanced vertical launch system.

Separate contract awards were also envisioned to go to United Defense, L.P., for the Advanced Gun System and to Alstom for the Integrated Power System.

The loss of the design agent organizational construct and the separation of the ship construction and combat systems development constituted a major change in program management structure. The design agent construct was intended to facilitate system integration by industry. This change leaves no single corporation clearly responsible for total ship system integration. The combat systems developer (Raytheon) retained some degree of systems integration responsibility, but the program office will now be placed in the role of total ship system integrator (as it has been on the AEGIS destroyer program).

The Congressional Response

Congress issued a very strong negative response with regard to the proposed competitive strategy. Senators from states in which both shipyards have facilities protested the plan, arguing that maintaining two shipyards capable of building surface combatants was vital to national security and that the winner-take-all approach would result in the loss of one of those shipyards.

Language in the FY 2005 Emergency Supplemental bill prohibited the winner-take-all shipyard competition strategy ("DD[X] Media Roundtable," 2005, slide 22). The FY 2006 DoD Authorization Act reported out by the Senate Armed Services Committee includes similar language.

The Proposed Compromise

In response to the congressional language, the Navy developed another strategy that attempted to balance the various political, budgetary, and programmatic interests. This compromise proposal envisions dual sole-source contracts to NGSS and BIW for lead ship design and construction—essentially two lead ships ("DD[X] Media Roundtable," 2005, slide 23). Each shipyard would do its own production design and purchase combat and power systems from the system developers as contractor-furnished equipment. Ship fabrication would begin in both shipyards in FY 2007. In FY 2009, a competition would be held for the follow ships; the form of this competition would be determined in FY 2008. This strategy delays the start of lead ship fabrication by eight months, from the forth quarter in FY 2007 to the third quarter in FY 2008.

The rationale behind this revised plan is similar to the plan laid out in April 2005. The Navy's analysis indicates that apportionment of one ship per year between two shipyards is not sufficient to maintain the workforce in the two shipyards. With a DD(X) class size estimated at 10 ships, CG(X) starting in FY 2011, and no more than two surface combatants per year in long-range plans, a different strategy was required. The Navy is aware that if NGSS wins the competition in FY 2009, there is currently no work projected for BIW, resulting in the potential loss of competition for the CG(X). If BIW wins, however, the Navy believes that the NGSS workload is sufficient to maintain a viable workforce and provide competition for CG(X).

This scheme calls for sole-source contracts to be awarded to the system and software developers in support of transitioning those systems to production. Software would be provided to the shipyards as government-furnished information.

The implied management structure again places the main system integration function with the Navy program office.

As of early July 2005, this acquisition strategy had been approved by the Assistant Secretary of the Navy for Research, Development, and Acquisition and sent to the USD(AT&L) for review and approval.

DDG 51–Class Case Study

Study Scope

The primary goal of this case study was to learn lessons about acquisition and contracting strategies that could be applicable to the DD(X) program. It is not intended to be an all-encompassing historical documentation of the DDG 51 program. The study was particularly focused on the Navy's and the program office's experience of handling the programmatic challenges created by the desire to achieve competition between the two shipbuilders, Bath Iron Works (BIW) and Ingalls, while complying with Navy policy to keep both shipbuilders in business.

Program Background

The DDG 51 destroyer class is one of the longest acquisition programs of its kind in U.S. Navy history. It started with its lead ship procurement in FY 1985 and is currently scheduled to deliver 62 ships, with the last procurement of three ships in FY 2005. This program has evolved through the years and encompasses three flights of ship hulls and eight combat system baselines.[1] BIW (currently part of General Dynamics Corp.) and Ingalls Shipbuilding (currently part of Northrop Grumman Ship Systems [NGSS]) are the two shipbuilders.

---

[1] The DDG 51 Program Office uses "flight" to define a hull configuration and "baseline" to define a combat system configuration.

The combat system is provided by several firms, including Lockheed Martin, Raytheon, United Defense, L3 Communications, General Dynamics, and others to the U.S. Navy, which in turn plays a key role as supplier of government-furnished equipment (GFE). The Navy procures the combat system from these companies as GFE and provides it to the shipbuilders.

The CG 47 class of cruisers preceded the DDG 51 destroyer class. Both classes of ships feature the Aegis combat system, which was designed primarily to provide air defense to the carrier battle group against large-scale attacks. Aegis cruisers were built starting in the late 1970s, with the last five ships authorized in FY 1988. All 27 Aegis cruisers were built at Ingalls or BIW.

The DDG 51 was designed to be a less-expensive and scaled-down version of a CG 47–class cruiser. The destroyer was intended to supplement the cruiser in defense of carrier battle groups on the open ocean. The DDG 51 is somewhat smaller in displacement, has fewer vertical launch system (VLS) cells, and was initially designed without organic helicopter capability. The DDG 51 combat system has fewer missiles and fire-control channels but in other respects has more capability than its predecessor, including a new and complex ship design. The ship's design incorporates features to increase its ability to survive during battle. Survivability features include a seakeeping hull; all-steel construction; armor in vital spaces; improved fire-fighting equipment; noise and infrared suppression systems and ship design to reduce radar cross section; and a collective protection system to guard the crew against contaminated air from nuclear, biological, and chemical agents.

Critical Requirements and Program Objectives Specified for the New System

A primary objective in addition to the survivability features described above was cost.

> The feasibility studies phase of the DDG(X) began in February 1980 with direction from CNO to obtain follow ship cost of $500 million (FY 1980 dollars) [or just over $900 million per

unit in FY 2003 dollars]. After a thorough in-house review of the various DDG 51 configurations, NAVSEA [Naval Sea Systems Command] recommended a gas turbine configuration of slightly under 8,500 long tons. Following [Office of Naval Operations] concurrence, NAVSEA started Preliminary Design in February 1982 and completed it in December 1982. The Preliminary Design was revised to incorporate changes to DDG 51 characteristics promulgated by [the Secretary of the Navy] in February 1983. In addition [the Secretary of the Navy] established cost thresholds. (Riddick, 2002.)

The Aegis combat system had already been developed and therefore was not a risk item. However, the incorporation of the collective protection system and stealthy design were risk items in ship construction. The Navy involved industry in preliminary design work to mitigate risk. In March 1983, NAVSEA directed that the contract design be conducted in-house rather than by a shipyard.

Contract Design started in May 1983 with a collocated Navy/industry team consisting of NAVSEA, shipbuilders, naval architecture and marine engineering firms, the Combat System Engineering Agent, and the Naval Surface Warfare Centers. To keep DDG 51 on schedule and within cost constraints, a Destroyer Management Review board (DMRB) was established by [the Secretary of the Navy]. The DMRB met bimonthly to review the Contract Design progress and procurement strategy to achieve performance and cost thresholds. Contract Design was completed June 29, 1984. (Riddick, 2003.)

Table A.1 shows differences between the later ships of the CG 47 class and the DDG 51 class. Both classes were upgraded over time and so have multiple configurations within each class.

Milestone dates for the DDG 51 are shown in Table A.2.

Key durations for the DDG 51 lead ship are shown in Table A.3, with comparison to the DD 963 lead ship. The CG 47 lead ship offers a poor comparison because it was a modified repeat built on the DD-963 hull, which was also built by Ingalls.

Table A.1
Comparison of Later Ships of CG 47 Class with DDG 51–Class Features

	CG 47 Class[a]	DDG 51 Flight I	DDG 51 Flight II	DDG 51 Flight IIA
Length of ship	567 feet	505 feet	505 feet	509 feet
Crew size	364	323	323	323
Weight, full load	9,600 tons	8,315 tons	8,400 tons	9,200 tons
VLS cells	122	90	96	96
Five-inch guns	2	1	1	1

[a]From CG-51 on.

Table A.2
DDG 51 Milestone Dates

Milestone	Date
Concept design completed	December 1980
Preliminary design completed	March 1983
Contract design completed	June 1984
Lead ship detail design and construction contract award	April 1985
Lead ship start fabrication	September 1987
Follow ship contract awarded to Ingalls	May 1987
Lead ship keel laid	December 1988
Lead ship launch	September 1989
Lead ship deliver	April 1991

Table A.3
Key Durations for DDG 51

	DDG 51	DD 963
Detail design contract award to start construction	29 months	
Detail design contract award to keel laid	44 months	29 months
Start construction to lead ship delivery	43 months	
Detail design contract award to lead ship delivery	72 months	62 months

BIW won the contract for detailed design and construction of the DDG 51–class lead ship in a competitive award. Todd and Ingalls also bid for the contract. A Fixed-Price Incentive (FPI) contract was used in accordance with direction from Navy leadership.

The Navy used a fixed-price detail design and lead ship construction contract to make the contractor bear more of the risk of meeting the target cost. The Navy kept competing contractors informed of design progress on the lead ship because it was the Navy's intention to compete subsequent ships and thereby help control costs. A competitive FPI contract was awarded to Ingalls to build the follow ship (DDG 52) in May 1987, and an FPI contract to build DDG 53 was awarded to BIW in September 1987. Workload at the Bath and Ingalls shipyards was maintained during this time by awards of CG 47–class ships through FY 1988. The overlap of CG 47–class construction with DDG 51, and the relatively modest concurrency of detail design (funded with the lead ship contract) and follow ship construction in the DDG 51 class are shown in Table A.4. Note that 11 CG 47–class ships were authorized in FYs 1986 through 1988 after the award of the DDG 51. This ongoing surface combatant work allowed the Navy to award no DDG 51–class ships in FYs 1986 and 1988 and to minimize concurrency between design and construction.

Table A.5 shows the award of DDG 51 hulls by fiscal year and yard and the award date, start of fabrication date, delivery date, and commissioning date for each ship. The duration in months from start of fabrication to delivery is calculated for each ship. The shaded areas are planned and subject to change (Department of the Navy, 2004).

System Integration in the DDG 51 Program

In the DDG 51 program, no single prime contractor has total responsibility for delivering a complete weapon system to the Navy.

Table A.4
Overlap of CG 47 and DDG 51–Class Construction
(Ships Awarded per Fiscal Year)

	FY 1984	FY 1985	FY 1986	FY 1987	FY 1988	FY 1989
CG 47	3	3	3	3	5	0
DDG 51	0	1	0	2	0	5
Total	3	4	3	5	5	5

Table A.5
Key Dates for Construction of DDG 51–Class Ships

Hull	Yard	Year Authorized	Award	Start Fabrication	Keel Laid	Delivery	Commissioned	Months from Fabrication to Delivery	Flight I	Flight II	Flight IIA
51	BIW	1985	Apr-85	Sep-87	Dec-88	Apr-91	Jul-91	43	X		
52	ISI	1987	May-87	May-89	Feb-90	Oct-92	Dec-92	41	X		
53	BIW	1987	Sep-87	Apr-89	Aug-90	Aug-93	Dec-93	52	X		
54	BIW	1989	Dec-88	May-90	Mar-91	Dec-93	Mar-94	43	X		
55	ISI	1989	Dec-88	Oct-90	Aug-91	May-94	Aug-94	43	X		
56	BIW	1989	Dec-88	Nov-90	Sep-91	May-94	Jul-94	42	X		
57	ISI	1989	Dec-88	Apr-91	Feb-92	Oct-94	Dec-94	42	X		
58	BIW	1989	Dec-88	May-91	Mar-92	Dec-94	Mar-95	43	X		
59	ISI	1990	Feb-90	Sep-91	Jul-92	Mar-95	May-95	42	X		
60	BIW	1990	Feb-90	Nov-91	Aug-92	Mar-95	May-95	40	X		
61	ISI	1990	Feb-90	Jan-92	Jan-93	May-95	Jul-95	40	X		
62	BIW	1990	Feb-90	May-92	Feb-93	Jul-95	Oct-95	38	X		
63	ISI	1990	Feb-90	Jul-92	May-93	Jul-95	Oct-95	36	X		
64	BIW	1991	Jan-91	Oct-92	Aug-93	Dec-95	Apr-96	38	X		
65	ISI	1991	Jan-91	Dec-92	Sep-93	Dec-95	Mar-96	36	X		
66	BIW	1991	Jan-91	Apr-93	Feb-94	Jun-96	Oct-96	38	X		
67	ISI	1991	Jan-91	May-93	Feb-94	Mar-96	Jun-96	34	X		
68	BIW	1992	Apr-92	Sep-93	Jul-94	Nov-96	Apr-97	38	X		
69	ISI	1992	Apr-92	Oct-93	Aug-94	Aug-96	Nov-96	34	X		
70	BIW	1992	Apr-92	Feb-94	Feb-95	Apr-97	Sep-97	38	X		
71	ISI	1992	Apr-92	Jun-94	Apr-95	Apr-97	Jun-97	34	X		
72	BIW	1992	Apr-92	Jul-94	Aug-95	Aug-97	Feb-98	37		X	
73	BIW	1993	Jan-93	Jan-95	Jan-96	Mar-98	Aug-98	38		X	
74	ISI	1993	Jan-93	Apr-95	Jan-96	Feb-98	Apr-98	34		X	

Table A.5—continued

Hull	Yard	Year Authorized	Award	Start Fabrication	Keel Laid	Delivery	Commissioned	Months from Fabrication to Delivery	Flight I	Flight II	Flight IIA
75	BIW	1993	Jan-93	Jun-95	Jul-96	Aug-98	Dec-98	38		X	
76	BIW	1993	Jan-93	Oct-95	Nov-96	Jan-99	Apr-99	39		X	
77	BIW	1994	Jul-94	Mar-96	May-97	May-99	Oct-99	38		X	
78	ISI	1994	Jul-94	Feb-96	Dec-96	Jan-99	Mar-99	35		X	
79	BIW	1994	Jul-94	Sep-96	Oct-97	May-00	Aug-00	44			X
80	ISI	1995	Jan-95	Mar-97	Dec-97	Jun-00	Oct-00	39			X
81	BIW	1995	Jan-95	Mar-97	May-98	Oct-00	Mar-01	43			X
82	ISI	1995	Jan-95	Oct-97	Aug-98	Feb-01	Apr-01	40			X
83	BIW	1996	Jun-96	Nov-97	Dec-98	Jun-01	Oct-01	43			X
84	ISI	1996	Jun-96	Jul-98	May-99	Aug-01	Dec-01	37			X
85	BIW	1997	Dec-96	Jul-98	Jul-99	Mar-02	Aug-02	44			X
86	ISI	1997	Dec-96	Jan-99	Dec-99	Feb-02	Jun-02	38			X
87	BIW	1997	Dec-96	Dec-98	Jan-00	Nov-02	Apr-03	47			X
88	ISI	1997	Dec-96	Sep-99	Jun-00	Aug-02	Nov-02	35			X
89	NGSS	1998	Mar-98	Jan-00	Jan-01	Apr-03	Feb-03	37			X
90	BIW	1998	Mar-98	Jun-99	Apr-01	May-03	Aug-03	50			X
91	NGSS	1998	Mar-98	May-00	Jul-01	Oct-03	Oct-03	41			X
92	BIW	1998	Mar-98	Mar-00	Nov-01	Mar-04	Apr-04	49			X
93	NGSS	1999	Mar-98	Mar-01	Jan-02	Mar-04	Mar-04	36			X
94	BIW	1999	Mar-98	Feb-01	Sep-02	Sep-04	Oct-04	44			X
95	NGSS	1999	Mar-98	Sep-01	Jul-02	Aug-04	Aug-04	35			X
96	BIW	2000	Mar-98	Sep-01	May-03	May-05	Jun-05	45			X
97	NGSS	2000	Mar-98	Mar-02	Jan-03	Jan-05	Jan-05	34			X
98	NGSS	2000	Mar-98	Sep-02	Aug-03	Aug-05	Aug-05	35			X
99	BIW	2001	Mar-98	Apr-02	Jan-04	Jan-06	Jan-06	45			X

Table A.5—continued

Hull	Yard	Year Authorized	Award	Start Fabrication	Keel Laid	Delivery	Commis- sioned	Months from Fabrication to Delivery	Flight I	Flight II	Flight IIA
100	NGSS	2001	Mar-98	Mar-03	Apr-04	Jan-06	Mar-06	36			X
101	BIW	2001	Mar-98	Feb-03	Aug-04	Sep-06	Aug-06	42			X
102	BIW	2002	Sep-02	Sep-03	Apr-05	Mar-07	Mar-07	42			X
103	NGSS	2002	Sep-02	Jun-04	Mar-04	Apr-07	Apr-07	34			X
104	BIW	2002	Sep-02	Apr-04	Nov-05	Nov-07	Nov-07	43			X
105	NGSS	2003	Sep-02	Mar-05	Mar-06	Jun-08	Mar-08	36			X
106	BIW	2003	Sep-02	Oct-04	Jul-06	Jul-08	Jun-08	44			X
107	NGSS	2004	Sep-02	TBD	TBD	Jun-09	TBD				X
108	BIW	2004	Sep-02	TBD	TBD	Feb-09	TBD				X
109	BIW	2004	Sep-02	TBD	TBD	Oct-09	TBD				X
110	NGSS	2005	Sep-02	TBD	TBD	Jun-10	TBD				X
111	BIW	2005	Sep-02	TBD	TBD	May-10	TBD				X
112	BIW	2005	Sep-02	TBD	TBD	Dec-10	TBD				X

Note: Shaded dates are scheduled.

The shipyards are responsible for delivering the basic ship (hull, mechanical systems, and electrical systems), but the Navy supplies the Aegis combat system to be installed in the ship. For this reason, it was necessary to create an organization responsible for overall integration of the combat system and the ship system. This system integration is performed by an "Aegis infrastructure" that comprises Lockheed Martin, Navy personnel, and many smaller contractors. How this process worked, and how much it cost, is of interest because a comparable process might be employed in the DD(X) program.

How Systems Integration Was Performed in DDG 51

The program manager assigns roles in select areas to the lead systems integrator. On DDG 51, the role was defined for the combat system. The integrator's role is to make sure that all the elements of the combat system work in harmony, perform their mission, fit on the ship, and meet specifications for power, cooling, volume, access, etc. The integrator also ensures that the design meets the weapon system's top-level requirements. Lockheed Martin performs this role on DDG 51. The role affects the shipbuilder because Lockheed must review designs by the yard that interface with the combat system.

The DDG 51 program provides shipbuilding funds to other Navy and joint participating managers to procure the GFE that is installed on new-construction DDGs. These funds are provided using Ship Project Directives that specify what material is to be procured, what quantity is to be procured, when and where the material is to be delivered, and how much funding will be provided. More than 2,500 line items of material from more than 40 participating managers are delivered for each DDG. It is possible that on another shipbuilding program, the Navy could decide to give some of the Navy's role in overseeing GFE to a contractor.

The DDG 51–class shipbuilding contracts include a series of attachments known as Schedules A through E. The attachments spell out the government's responsibility for delivery dates, specifications, etc., for GFE. If the government is late or provides incompatible data or equipment or otherwise fails to meet its responsibilities as specified in the contract, the shipbuilder may be entitled to compensation. There has never been an instance of either shipbuilder submitting a claim to the government for late GFE on the DDG 51 program, although it has been a problem on other shipbuilding programs. The consistent on-time delivery of material and information and lack of problems stem from the support infrastructure, including systems integration, which has been created to support the Aegis program.

The systems integration contract with Lockheed is a cost plus award fee contract that has a base year with options for renewal.

In summary, the government and the contractors perform systems integration, broadly defined, in the DDG 51 program, each with areas of specific responsibilities.

What Portion of Total DDG 51 Program Costs Can Be Allocated to System Integration?

We wanted to identify these costs to serve as a basis to quantify the integration costs in the DD(X) program. Unfortunately, our discussions with program office personnel suggested such a task to be extremely difficult because the integration costs in the DDG 51 program are spread among Navy-furnished material, Aegis costs, and shipbuilding costs, as shown in Figure A.1. These three major costs are averaged over the life of the program as they appear in the budget. Here, shipbuilding costs account for slightly less than half the total ship cost. Navy-furnished material is all electronics and ordnance equipment that is not part of the Aegis combat system. In the budget, the cost of systems integration is spread among these categories/items and does not appear explicitly. Systems integration is performed by the "Aegis infrastructure" that comprises Lockheed Martin, Navy personnel, and many smaller contractors.

According to the program office, the Lockheed Martin system integration contract cost averages 6 percent of GFE cost over time. This figure includes the cost of the Lockheed Martin system integration contract, which does not include such other functions as test, software modifications to ensure system interoperability, or cost of other organizations that are part of the "Aegis infrastructure."

Figure A.1
Distribution of Total DDG 51 Ship Costs in Budget

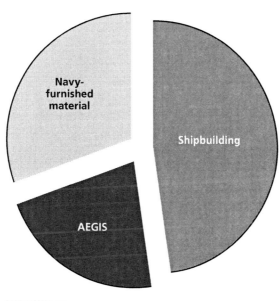

How Ongoing Development Within the Class Affected the Shipbuilders and Vendors

The DDG 51 class was planned as an acquisition program with continuous incremental capability upgrades in its acquisition strategy document, Decision Coordinating Paper (DCP) 1337, dated December 15, 1983. DCP 1337 envisioned that the class would be upgraded in flights. Changes in configuration to the hull are termed flights, and changes in the combat system are termed baselines. The hull has been built in three flights, and the combat system is now in its eighth baseline. Hull flights are shown in Table A.6.

Flight IIA ships added the organic capability for two SH-60 Light Airborne Multipurpose System helicopters and the Recovery Assist Securing and Traversing system, among other improvements.

Table A.6
DDG 51–Class Flights

Hull Flight	Fiscal Year Authorized	Hull Number	Number of Ships
Flight I	1985–1992	DDG 51–71	21
Flight II	1992–1994	DDG 72–78	7
Flight IIA	1994–2005	DDG 79–112	34

The flight changes to the hull affected primarily the shipbuilders, while the baseline changes to the combat systems affected primarily the combat system contractors, with mostly minor effects on the shipbuilders. A few of the combat system baseline changes had major effects on the shipbuilders.

Baseline upgrades to the combat system are shown in Table A.7.Design work on changes to the hull is funded on the lead yard services contract. Among the more significant upgrades has been addition of two helicopter hangers on the aft deck in Flight IIA. To save costs, this capability was not included in the original design because it was thought that the DDGs would accompany the carrier battle group with other ships that had helicopter hangers. With the end of the Cold War and more independent operation of DDG 51–class ships, it became more desirable to have organic helicopter capability on the ships.

Later combat system upgrades on Flight IIA ships incorporate Cooperative Engagement Capability to network air defenses among various platforms and Extended-Range Guided Munitions on the five-inch gun, among other upgrades. These major improvements underscore the versatility of the DDG 51 because they are in virtually every area of naval warfare—strike, antisurface, antisubmarine, and antiair capability and naval gunfire support.

The changes to the hull and combat systems had noteworthy consequences for the warfighters, for the contractors, and for analysts attempting to derive lessons from the program. For the warfighters, the flight changes added warfighting capability in an incremental fashion as intended. The DDG 51–class destroyer is the most capable

Table A.7
DDG 51–Class Combat System Upgrades

Combat System Baseline	Fiscal Year Authorized	Hull Number	Number of Ships
4 Phase I	1985–1987	DDG 51–53	3
4 Phase II	1989	DDG 54–58	5
5 Phase I	1990–1991	DDG 59–67	9
5 Phase III	1992–1994	DDG 68–78	11
6 Phase I	1994–1996	DDG 79–84	6
6 Phase III	1997–1998	DDG 85–90	6
7 Phase I	1998–2001	DDG 91–101	11
7 Phase IR	2002–2005	DDG 102–112	11

surface combatant afloat, and the baseline upgrades regularly add to this capability in littoral and open ocean environments.

For the contractors, an important consequence of the upgrades is that the changes have provided a stream of planning and design work to the contractors during the life of the program. This ongoing work has preserved the ship and combat system design and engineering base that will be crucial for the next surface combatant. The ship design contracts are a more stable source of profits on a percentage basis than shipbuilding contracts. Design contracts are cost plus a 10 percent fee (3 percent fixed, 7 percent award fee), while profits on shipbuilding contracts vary considerably and can be in the low single digits for the costlier shipyard under the current contracting arrangement.

Despite the multiple upgrades, the DDG 51 program has been successful in maintaining its unit cost over the past two decades. This in itself is a remarkable achievement for the program. Unfortunately, these incremental upgrades or changes make it difficult for analysts to measure the effects of acquisition strategies on cost because the unit being measured is constantly changing. Analysts often compare the improvement or learning curve of the cost of individual ships in a program to the cost improvement on other programs with different acquisition strategies to assess cost effects. Changes in capability and cost make assessing the cost improvement difficult over the life of the program because each change tends to disrupt learning and the changed configuration results in a new baseline for further cost improvement. Changes in the procurement rate per year further complicate the analysis because costs per unit change with rate. Thus it is difficult to compare the cost history of this program to that of other shipbuilding programs or to assess the effect of acquisition or contracting strategies on cost.

In summary, the Navy's acquisition strategy over the length of the DDG 51 program has contributed to stability in the surface combatant business base while using competition and contractual incentives to control cost and maximize performance. The program has been able to take advantage of technological advances leading to increased capabilities in multiple flights. Advances in combat system capabilities may have paralleled the cost reductions in the computer industry, thereby allowing significant improvements in capability while holding costs constant over time.

Contracting Strategies and Their Impact on Design Transfer and Competition

Over the duration of the acquisition program, the DDG 51 Program Office has continuously evolved its contracting strategies to get the best price, encourage competition between the two shipbuilding contractors, and maintain the industrial base. Achieving these often-conflicting goals has been difficult, as yearly ship procurements have declined to an average of three per year. A summary of contracting strategies is shown in Table A.8.

Under the "Competition" phase, BIW won the competition for detail design and for building the lead ship in FY 1985. Ingalls won

Table A.8
Changing Contracting Strategies on the DDG 51 Class

Contracting Strategy	Fiscal Year	Hull Number	Number of Ships
Competition	1985–1993	DDG 51–76	26
Negotiated Allocation	1994–1995	DDG 77–82	6
Profit Related to Offer	1996–1997	DDG 83–88	6
Multiyear Procurement	1998–2005	DDG 89–112	24

the contract to build the follow ship in FY 1987, and BIW won the contract to build the other ship authorized in FY 1987. The intense competition for work led to aggressive bids in an effort to get it. Those bids subsequently proved to be low, leading to significant cost increases on these FPI contracts. The use of FPI contracts on development or high-risk production efforts would not be acceptable in the current environment (partly as a result of the DDG 51 experience), where the present accepted practice is to use Cost Plus Incentive contracts until the design details are completed and finalized. The contractor bears less cost risk on a cost-type contract than on a fixed-price contract, but this is the trade-off that must be made to allow continuous production while design details are being completed.

Beginning in FY 1989, the program office began procuring five ships per year split between the two contractors. The government was interested in keeping both yards operating to alleviate industrial base concerns. The industrial base authority in 10 USC 2304 permitted an award pattern that was not the lowest cost combination of offers in order to maintain balanced sources of supply. For instance, in FY 1990 when five ships were appropriated, each shipbuilder submitted bids to construct one, two, three, and four ships. The lowest cost combination would have been a four-one award pattern. However, that pattern would have created an imbalance in workload between the yards and the one-ship award to the loser would have created instability in the loser's workforce. This instability would have led to efficiency problems, and if the lowest cost award pattern continued year after year, both shipyards would have experienced production inefficiencies arising from hiring and firing cycles caused by an unstable business base. To maintain a stable business base, the five ships in FY 1990 were awarded in a three-two split at a slightly higher cost than the four-one split.

From the contractors' perspective, the two shipyards were aware that the government was interested in keeping both their yards alive. The situation allowed a yard to bid high, and as the loser of the yearly competition build one or probably two ships at a higher contract target price per ship and make a higher profit per ship than the winner of the competition. Although maximizing total profit and workload are probably more compelling motivations for a shipyard's bidding behavior than profit percentage is, instances of the losing yard making a higher profit per ship than the winning yard occurred during this time. Recognizing this problem, the Assistant Secretary of the Navy decided to allocate the ships to the two contractors in FY 1994 and FY 1995, while researching ways to enhance competition between them. This contracting strategy is termed "negotiated allocation," wherein the government negotiates the contract with each shipbuilder individually to ensure a reasonable target cost and profit. This approach recognized that each shipbuilder's target cost is a function of its manufacturing process, business base, and labor rates and productivity. The labor rates and productivity differences reflect regional differences between the locations of the two yards and are difficult if not impossible to change, giving one yard an inherent advantage in competition. The allocation approach acknowledged the cost differences between the yards and sought to negotiate a fair profit for each yard, without creating the incentive for higher bids of the previous approach. Allocation also fulfilled the Navy's policy of keeping surface combatant construction at both yards.

Beginning in FY 1996, the "Profit Related to Offer" (PRO) concept was introduced in an effort to rejuvenate competition. The PRO concept used profit as a means of competition between the two contractors while allowing each contractor to bid realistically on target cost. The profit would be set at a certain percentage for the winning contractor that submitted the lower bid, and the losing contractor's profit percentage would be decreased in proportion to how much higher his target cost was compared to that of the winner. Figure A.2 shows how the PRO concept was designed to work.

As shown in Figure A.2, both contractors were asked to bid target costs only. The winner received a predetermined target profit percentage, with a 50-50 share line if actual costs exceeded the target cost. The loser's profit percentage was based on the winner's profit percentage and adjusted down in proportion to the difference between the loser's and winner's target costs using a mathematical

Figure A.2
An Illustration of the PRO Concept

PRO example

- Each yard awarded equal number of ships
- Total procurement must be an even number of ships
- Each yard bids target cost only
- Contract ceiling value established after bids are submitted

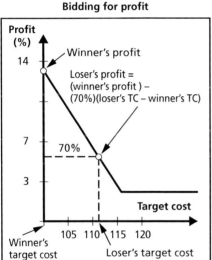

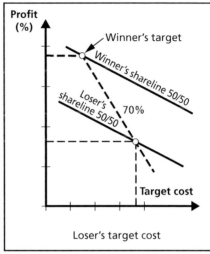

formula. Such a system was designed to ensure that the two contractors are not penalized in their share of the work for their differences in costs. On the DDG 51 program, BIW has higher costs than Ingalls because manufacturing processes, labor forces, and business bases make it more expensive to build ships at BIW than at Ingalls. This contracting strategy allows both contractors to bid at and recover their costs but favors the contractor with lower target cost to get the higher profit. From the government's perspective, such a concept minimizes the deviation in the total price (target cost plus profit) between the two contractors. Both contractors followed a predetermined government-contractor share line for under and over target cost scenarios with a contract ceiling value established after the bids were submitted. The PRO concept was later extended into a multiyear procurement contract beginning in FY 1998. This ensured greater stability in the business base for the two contractors.

PRO has been used in conjunction with multiyear procurement over the last eight years of the program (FY 1998–2005). Multiyear procurement has given the shipyards a greater sense of assurance of future work, and has allowed them to approach their vendors with economic order quantity bids over several years. This process of stabilization of workload has enabled the contractors to invest in multiple capital improvement projects, which require an initial non-recurring investment in time and money, but which provide long-term rewards by allowing the two contractors to develop innovative technologies to lower costs and save money.

The DDG 51 program has maintained an FPI contracting strategy throughout the program, beginning with the lead ship built by BIW and the follow ship built by Ingalls. The FPI contracts were based on a fixed share line below and above target cost wherein the government and contractor shared the overtarget costs and under-target costs on a predetermined share ratio. Beyond the Point of Total Assumption, the contractor assumed all the costs, as shown in Figure A.3. A 50-50 share ratio was used during the period FY 1985–FY 1995, wherein the costs below or above target were split 50-50 between the government and the contractor, respectively.[2] The share line was used as a means to share cost risk between the contractor and the government and to reward the contractor according to financial performance. This covered the "Competition for Work" and "Negotiated Allocation" periods.

With the passage of time and in addition to the introduction of the PRO concept, several variations were made to the FPI contracts in the form of incentives to the contractors. These variations were made as the program office obtained more information and intro-

---

[2] The original share line on the DDG 51 ship at time of award was 50-50. On September 15, 1989, ECP 760 revised the share line from 50-50 to 80-20.

Figure A.3
The Basic Elements in an FPI Contract

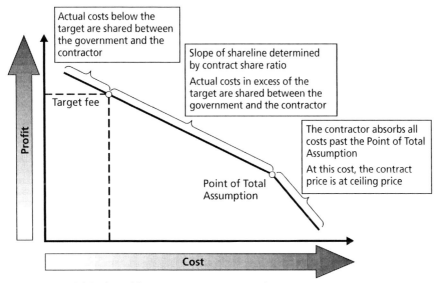

Risk is shared between government and contractor

duced innovative methods to motivate contractors to increase efficiency, using the contract vehicle. For instance, the undertarget share ratios were modified beyond FY 1995 to incentivize cost performance. The contractor's share of undertarget share ratio was made greater than the government's share to incentivize the contractors to get a bigger share of the savings. On the other hand, the overtarget share line was changed beginning in FY 2002 to reduce the government's share at 110 percent of target cost and to encourage more realistic bidding. The share ratios evolved from being the same for both contractors to being different as the program office obtained information on the limitations on target cost stemming from manufacturing process and business base issues unique to each contractor. Beginning in FY 1996, the contract ceiling price was transitioned to a random selection process to promote realistic bidding and prevent share-line gaming of bids between the contractors.

Award fees of up to $10 million additional profit per ship on shipbuilding contracts were used to motivate the contractors in technical and management performance areas specified in the contract. The program office personnel believed this to be a very effective tool in motivating the contractors to behave in ways beneficial to the government during the course of the contract. For instance, award fees were provided for specific aspects of contractor performance, such as achieving a milestone by a certain date. The award fees are reviewed and awarded every six months, which improves cash flow to the contractor.

Our discussions with current and former procurement contracting officers of the DDG 51 Program Office suggest that these fees must be carefully assigned to clearly defined measurable outcomes and not provide additional awards for the contractors on completing deliverables already written into the contract. Such a practice would prevent contractors from taking these award fees for granted and using them as means to adjust their bids on target cost.

Considering this historical experience in the context of the DD(X) program, an FPI contract is not recommended for a lead ship design and construction. Additionally, a flexible contracting strategy is recommended wherein the terms of the contract could be altered periodically to minimize cost, schedule, and performance risks to the program as the industrial base and DoD needs evolve.

Impact on Design Transfer

We asked the program office and the procurement contracting officers whether any issues cropped up related to transfer of design from the lead ship builder to the follow ship builder and/or when there were flight changes. Their response indicated that the lead ship designer was contractually responsible for transferring the data to the follow ship builder according to a detailed schedule, with award fees to incentivize performance. As a result, the program office and shipbuilders did not encounter any major problems or delays related to design transfer except as a result of concurrent detail design and construction on the lead and first two follow ships.

For the lead and first two follow ships, there was a problem with the timing of lead ship construction and the award of the follow ships while detail design was in progress and before actual cost data were available. The scope of the contract on the second ship was adjusted after a few years, after the detail design was complete and actual costs were incurred. The last Selected Acquisition Reports (SARs) for each contract show large increases in target cost on the lead and next two follow ships, indicating that the government acknowledged contractually that aggressive cost performance projected by the contractors and reflected in their bids were not realized. This may indicate that the shipyards could not accurately estimate the cost of the ships when they submitted their bids for the follow ships, that the yards knowingly bid aggressively in an extremely competitive environment, or that the government added work scope to the original contract. In any event, the contracting officers and other program office personnel believe that having detail design complete before soliciting bids for follow ships would be ideal. This ideal is impractical because of the need for continuous production to maintain shipyard workforces. However, advances in design tools and management practices, such as Integrated Product and Process Development, in which design and construction personnel work as a team to develop a construction-friendly design, may reduce the risks in concurrency.

Despite cost overruns on the first three ships of the DDG 51 class and the belief of knowledgeable officials that it would be best to minimize concurrency between design and construction, the Navy's cost estimate of the DDG 51 provides evidence that accurately estimating the cost of a lead ship is possible.

The information in Table A.9[3] shows that the original Navy independent estimate for the DDG 51 detail design and construction cost was slightly higher than, but close to, the final cost at ship delivery. The number in the President's Budget submitted in January 1984 was lower than the original estimate and reflected the total ship

---

[3] Provided by Jerry Cantor, PMS-400, via e-mail in October 2003.

Table A.9
Track of DDG 51 Cost Estimates from Initial Estimate to Ship Delivery
(then-year $ million)

P-5 Budget Exhibit Categories	Navy Independent Estimate	President's Budget 1985	Contract Award	Budget at Delivery
Plans	157	125	119	189
Basic construction	418	379	216	337
Change orders	33	38	28	84
Escalation	73	76	52	50
Total shipbuilding	681	618	415	660
GFE	568	555	651	558
Other	39	25	25	28
PMG	57	54	38	0
End cost	1,345	1,252	1,129	1,246

cost of $1.25 billion, which was the cost goal for the lead ship established by the Secretary of the Navy. There was great pressure to stay within that total. In 1985, the DDG 51 budget was cut $123 million by Congress to reflect the contract award at BIW from the $1.252 billion in the President's Budget submitted in 1984. The $1.129 billion budget is shown in Table A.9 in the third column of numbers. In 1985, the Navy's policy was to budget for these contracts at target cost (bid). No budget was reserved for overtarget performance. By the time the lead ship was delivered, the budget had been increased to cover its final cost, which was below the original independent estimate and below the threshold set by the Secretary of the Navy.

The contracting officers also believed that on design contracts, one party must be held accountable legally and contractually. If other parties are involved, the government should ensure that they agree with the arrangement up front so that the government can maximize the probability that the arrangement will work.

Impact of Competition
In general the contracting strategy of the DDG 51 program might be described as fostering competition: first, competition for work share through a traditional price-based competition approach and, second, competition for profit though the PRO approach—all the while maintaining the industrial base. FPI contracts have been used

throughout the program for ship detail design and procurement, although cost plus award fee contracts have been used for lead yard services, follow yard services, and planning yard contracts.

It is difficult to analyze the effectiveness of competition in an environment where the contractors knew that the government was openly interested in keeping both shipyards in business, where yearly procurement quantities precluded much variation in work to the yards, and where the configuration of the ship and its combat system were constantly changing. The program office believes that if there were only one shipbuilder, cost improvement would flatten, thereby leading to higher costs compared to the actual program with two shipbuilders. This belief is shaped strongly by the experience of the CG 47–class procurement, described in Appendix B. On that program, Ingalls was the sole builder for the first several ships and little cost improvement occurred. The unit cost of the ships came down when BIW was introduced as the second builder.

The effect of competition on the cost of the DDG 51 class is less clear (see Figure A.4). One obvious effect of competition is aggressive bids and subsequent cost over target value on the FPI contracts, espe-

Figure A.4
DDG 51–Class Shipbuilding Costs per Unit (from SARs)

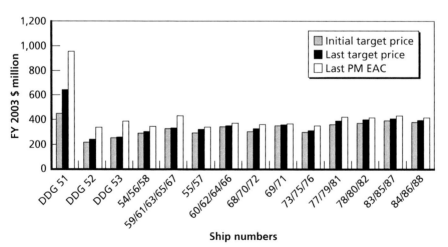

cially early in the program. This is shown by the difference in the height of each white bar, which is the last government program manager's estimate at completion (PM EAC), compared to the height of the black bar, which is the last negotiated target price of the contract reported in the SAR. The growth from the gray bar to the black bar indicates growth in cost negotiated between the government and the contractor since the contract award.

The cost improvement over the life of the program is less obvious. There is clearly a rate effect, in which years with only one or two ships built result in higher unit costs than years with four or five ships built. Overall, the unit costs have remained fairly stable over time, while the ships have grown in size and capability. In general, precisely quantifying the effects of competition on this program is impossible. One can only say that shipbuilding costs have remained fairly stable in constant dollars over many years. Regardless of the effect of competition, the stable unit cost of the ship over time is an impressive achievement given the reductions in quantities bought per year, the decline in the shipbuilding business base, the continuing improvements to the ship, and the cost growth experienced on other shipbuilding programs during the same period.

The data displayed in Figure A.5 tell a similar story. The data are taken from budget exhibits submitted by the Navy and show costs divided into three categories. Hull, mechanical, and electrical (HM&E) includes basic ship construction, planning, change orders, escalation, HM&E equipment, and other costs. This category includes the basic shipbuilding costs shown in Figure A.4 plus some other costs. The "electronics" category includes various sonar, electronic warfare, communications, and similar equipment. The category of "ordnance" is composed primarily of the Aegis weapon system, vertical launch system (VLS), five-inch gun, and other weapon systems. Figure A.5 shows that costs in each of the three categories have increased very slightly in constant dollars over ten years, and, when normalized for yearly rate, costs have remained constant. Again, especially considering that the data span five combat system baseline upgrades, this is an impressive achievement.

Figure A.5
DDG 51–Class Shipbuilding Costs per Unit (from FY 1998 through FY 2004 President's Budgets)

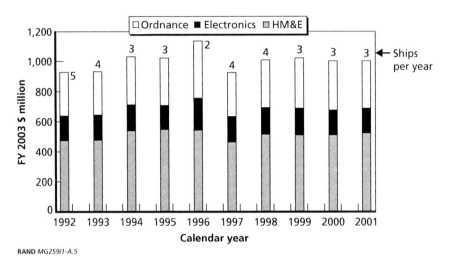

RAND *MG259/1-A.5*

The additional data shown in Figure A.5 also illustrate the difficulty in attributing the impressive cost performance to competition. Each of the three categories had stable costs. Most of the ordnance equipment is bought from sole-source suppliers today, although there is often competition among lower-tier vendors. In this area, the DDG 51 program may have benefited from the general progress in technology, from competition in related areas of weapons that led to improvements and cost reductions in weapons systems on the DDG 51 class, from competition among lower-tier vendors, and from competition among some first-tier vendors.

In summary, while the direct impact of competition is unclear, the long-term nature of the program has provided a stable business base to the two shipbuilders who have provided increasing capability over the years to the Navy at a stable unit cost. The Navy has continuously evolved its contracting strategy to minimize program cost and provide incentives for desired performance.

Conclusions

Several lessons suggest themselves from the DDG 51 shipbuilding program. One lesson that is widely if not universally recognized is the need to use cost type contracts for detail design and for ship construction on ships awarded until the design details are completed. Under these circumstances a transition to FPI type contracts is appropriate.

A second and related lesson is that high levels of concurrency between design and ship construction tends to lead to rework, cost growth in construction, and uncertainty about the true scope of construction work. It may be difficult to formulate realistic bids for ship construction while design is in progress, and some observers would say until substantial progress has been made on the lead ship construction. On the DDG 51 program, a one-year gap occurred between award of the lead ship and the next two ships. Even with this gap, the 29 months required for detail design meant that bids for the follow ships were formulated before the detail design was complete and construction on the lead ship began. Ideally there should be enough time between construction of the lead and follow ships that design problems discovered in lead ship construction can be redesigned and revised drawings provided to the follow ship builder. In reality, however, this is not a practical approach because of the loss of continuity in ship construction. Recent advances in design tools combined with management approaches implementing Integrated Process and Product Development teams of design and construction personnel may provide the optimum solution of developing a construction-friendly design while maintaining concurrency and continuity in the workforce.

A third and related lesson is that concurrency between the predecessor shipbuilding program and new shipbuilding program is desirable to provide stable work to the shipyards and to help mitigate concurrency between design and construction on the new program.

A fourth lesson is to continuously evolve contracting strategies to minimize cost, schedule, and performance risks to the program as the industrial base and needs of DoD change. The DDG 51 program has spanned 20 years of production, during which time the industrial base and warfighting needs of the Navy have changed. The Navy's acquisition and contracting strategies have successfully maintained two shipbuilders of surface combatants while providing higher performance at a stable unit cost over time.

Competition Effects in Recent Shipbuilding Programs

There is no easy way to quantify the effects of competition toward minimizing cost growth and schedule overruns and/or maximizing technical performance. In addition to the problem of quantifying the effects in any given situation, the effects are likely to vary depending on at least five factors. Among the factors that may determine the effects of competition on cost are the number of suppliers, the business environment in the particular industry, the minimum sustaining rate to keep a contractor in business, the production rate effect, and the competitive position between the contractors (Boger, Greer, and Lao, 1990). Despite the difficulties in quantifying the effects of competition, we examined the historical experience of several shipbuilding programs, including the TAO 187, LSD 41, CG 47, DDG 51, and LPD 17 class of ships, to get a better understanding of how competition might have played a role in their costs.

Characteristics of the U.S. Shipbuilding Industry

Given that the effects of competition on cost are likely to depend on at least the five characteristics listed above, the experience of historical programs can be applied to future programs with the most confidence when these characteristics are similar. The shipbuilding programs considered here were executed mostly during the 1980s and 1990s. If the characteristics in the shipbuilding industry during this period still obtain today, we can have greater confidence that the experience of these programs is relevant to DD(X).

Since the 1980s, the U.S. shipbuilding industry has been dependent on the government for subsidies for commercial ships or for orders for military ships. With the end of subsidies in the early 1980s, commercial shipbuilding all but vanished in the United States. Dozens of yards went out of business or consolidated during the 1980s and 1990s, and the industry became more highly concentrated. The U.S. Navy accounted for the vast majority of business in the industry throughout this period.

The characteristics in the shipbuilding industry today are similar to, but in some ways more extreme than they were in the 1980s. In terms of the five characteristics listed above:

- Fewer shipbuilders in total exist now, and, for most Navy ships, only one or two yards specialize in that class of ship. Only two yards build nuclear-powered submarines. Today, they share construction of one attack submarine per year. Only two yards build such large and complex surface combatants as cruisers and destroyers. One of these two yards is also the sole builder of large-deck amphibious ships. Auxiliary ships and smaller amphibious ships can be built in more yards. In general, most U.S. Navy ships are built at only one or two yards. Little overlap occurs among the specialty areas of the yards.

- It is easier to generalize about the competitiveness of shipbuilding market niches in the United States than about the industry as a whole. For niches in which two or more yards are capable of building a ship, including surface combatants, auxiliary ships, and smaller amphibious ships, yards tend to compete fiercely with each other for the business. For ship classes produced by only one yard, the shipyards, especially those with powerful representation in Congress, have less pressure to compete and control costs.

- In general, the minimum sustaining rate to keep a yard in business has become smaller as shipyards have reduced capacity to meet reduced demand. The specific minimum rate for each yard varies.

- It is difficult to generalize about the production rate effect across industries or across companies within an industry. It is logical to believe that the rate effect is unique to each company in relation to its business volume. In examining how average unit costs fluctuate with yearly changes in quantity on the DDG 51 program, it is apparent that a strong rate effect influences the yards involved. The only conclusion about how this might have changed in the shipbuilding industry over the last 20 to 25 years is that, given the decrease in capacity, the production rates must have smaller base quantities now than they did when shipyard capacities were greater.

- The competitive position between contractors is largely determined by labor costs because competing yards produce ships of the same design, with identical GFE and similar material costs. Labor costs are largely determined by wage rates and labor productivity that depend heavily on regional economic differences. Therefore, the competitive position between contractors in different regions is likely to remain the same over time. In the case of the shipyards for surface combatants, Ingalls has had and still enjoys a competitive advantage in labor costs over BIW.

To summarize the characteristics of the U.S. shipbuilding industrial base, there are fewer shipyards and less capacity now than in the 1980s, but for most classes of warships only one or two yards specialized in the class throughout most of the period. Competition for business remains strong because there is little other business.

TAO 187 Class of Ships

Acquisition of the TAO 187 class of auxiliary oiler ships had been competed from program inception in the early 1980s to the late 1980s in a series of three blocks (Pepper, 1989). The acquisition strategy consisted of two phases. The first phase brought in six qualified contractors who were awarded contracts to deliver proposals on design and construction of TAO in the second phase. Avondale won the FPI contract for Block I in FY 1982 as the lowest bidder for design and construction of the TAO 187 with the option for three more ships,[1] which were exercised by November 1983.

Proposals were solicited from five contractors in Block II for construction of nine TAO ships. The award was to be made to the lowest bidder in terms of overall target price. However, the government reserved the right to award one or more ships to an offeror other than the lowest bidder for mobilization purposes. This resulted in a split award where Penn Ship bid significantly lower than the other yards to win an FPI contract for two ships with option for two more, and Avondale won as the low bidder on the second FPI contract of one ship and the option to build two more.

Penn Ship's target prices were very optimistic in comparison to the Avondale prices on the first four ships. In FY 1988, Penn Ship had financial problems, causing them to propose a transfer of TAO 194 and TAO 196 to Avondale for completion. Navy approved the request, resulting in the final cost of the four ships at $17 million (in FY 1989 dollars) above the Penn Ship negotiated ceiling price.

The NCCA analyst estimated that competition saved the Navy in total production costs by comparing the projected sole-source costs based on cost improvement over the first four ships built by Avondale to the actual costs that resulted from competition.

The TAO program experience suggests that intense competition may cause contractors to underbid to win a contract. This may result in cost growth on the underbid contract, failure to achieve expected savings on the contract, and may contribute to less-efficient yards leaving the business and a declining industrial base. The experience also suggests that when total program quantities are sufficient to allow meaningful competition, cost savings can offset the costs of establishing a second source.

---

[1] The fifth ship was not awarded because of budget constraints.

LSD 41 Class of Ships

Acquisition of the LSD 41 class of ships began with Lockheed being competitively awarded a cost plus fixed fee contract in October 1978 for ship system design support, while being designated the lead ship-builder with sole-source production contracts for LSD 41, 42, and 43 during the period FY 1981 through FY 1983. After receiving a mature design package in FY 84, the Navy decided to compete LSD 44 and subsequent vessels. Six contractors submitted proposals, with Avondale topping the winner-take-all bidding for one ship in FY 1984, with options for two ships in FY 1985 and two in FY 1986. It is important to note that Avondale was willing to bid with lower-than-average profit of only 1.7 percent to win the contract.

Lockheed's response to competition for LSD 44 and beyond was to significantly reduce the proposed quote for production and engineering man-hours by 17 percent and 45 percent, respectively, from a projected estimate of the hours attainable through learning from the first three units. Once again, this behavior suggests that the contractor reduces price when exposed to competitive pressures.

Figure B.1 illustrates the drop in price between the third ship of the class, built by Lockheed, and the fourth ship of the class, built by Avondale. The unit prices of LSDs 45–48 continue to drop, although part of the reduction may stem from the rate effect at two ships per year.

CG 47 Class of Ships

The Navy awarded the lead ship of the class to Ingalls in 1978. The Navy awarded the next five follow ships to Ingalls in 1980, 1981, and 1982 on a sole-source basis. The cost improvement on the first six ships at Ingalls was not impressive. In 1982, the Navy awarded BIW the CG 51 as a second source. The Navy awarded the next three cruisers, CG 54 to CG 56, on a sole-source basis to Ingalls in 1983 but with a significant drop in unit price. The 1984 buy of three ships

Figure B.1
LSD 41–Class Shipbuilding Prices per Unit (from SARs)

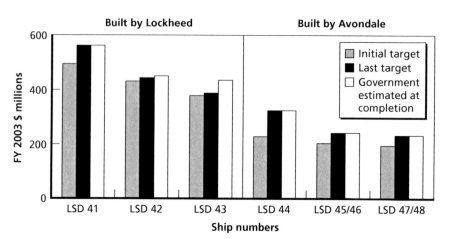

RAND MG259/1-B.1

was the first lot competed, and it resulted in a further significant reduction in the unit price. The government program manager's estimate at completion of the unit price of the first seven lots is shown in Figure B.2. The sharp drop in the unit price of Ingalls's ships is apparent after the introduction of BIW as a second source.

An analyst at the Naval Center for Cost Analysis calculated a significantly better rate of cost improvement at Ingalls after the introduction of BIW as a second source, and overall cost savings to the program despite the additional start up cost at Bath (Lo, 1985). The experience with the Aegis cruiser program was a powerful influence on the acquisition strategy for the follow-on Aegis surface combatant, the DDG 51 class.

DDG 51 Class

The experience with the DDG 51 class provides a less clear example of the consequences of competition. Unlike the first three programs examined, which followed periods of sole-source procurement with

Figure B.2
CG 47–Class Shipbuilding Prices per Unit (from SARs)

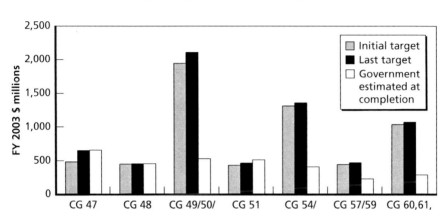

RAND *MG259/1-B.2*

competitive procurements, the acquisition strategy for the DDG 51 class was intended from the beginning to be based on competition. The contract for lead ship detail design and construction was competitively awarded to BIW in April 1985. It had bid aggressively because its CG 47 and FFG 7–class work was ending, and management believed that the company's survival depended on winning the contract. An FPI contract was used in accordance with direction from Navy leadership. The Navy used fixed-price detail design and lead ship construction contracts to force the contractor to bear more of the risk. An FPI contract was awarded to Ingalls to build the follow ship in May 1987, and an FPI contract to build DDG 53 was awarded to BIW in September 1987. Workload at the BIW and Ingalls shipyards was maintained during this time by ongoing awards of CG 47–class ships through FY 1988. The overlap of CG 47–class construction with the start of the DDG 51 program allowed relatively modest concurrency of detail design (funded with the lead ship contract) and follow ship construction in the DDG 51 class as well as adequate work for both yards.

The intense competition led to aggressive bidding by both yards. The lead ship contract and the first four follow ship contract awards overran their target price significantly. Budgets were set to the target price and then revised upward as overruns became apparent.

Obvious lessons consistent with the other programs described here are that contractors will bid aggressively in a competitive environment when they need work and that fixed-price contracts are inadvisable until the ship's design has stabilized.

Conclusions about the effect of competition on cost are less obvious for a number of reasons. Because two builders were involved for the entire program, it is not possible to compare a period of sole-source construction with a period of competition. Also, the DDG 51 program went through continuous upgrades to its hull and combat systems, which affected costs. Quantities per year after DDG 53 varied from two to five ships, making cost comparisons even more difficult. The strategy was modified over the life of the program from competition to allocation to a concept known as "profit related to offer" in which the profit of the higher bidder is cut in proportion to how much its cost exceeded that of the lower bidder. Given changes in configuration and reductions in rate per year, the relatively constant unit price under a strategy of dual sourcing does not look bad, especially in contrast to the LPD 17. Figure B.3 shows the DDG 51 program manager's estimates at completion for ships awarded through 1998, as reported in the final SAR for each contract.

Impressions about the effect of competition on cost are best made in comparison with the LPD 17 program. The LPD 17 program offers a suitable comparison because it is a relatively complex amphibious ship built by Ingalls and its sister yard, Avondale, but under an allocation scheme whereby Ingalls was to build two ships for every one built at BIW. That scheme has since been modified so that Ingalls and Avondale will build all the ships of the class.

LPD 17 Class

The lead ship contract for detail design and lead ship construction of LPD 17 is a cost-type contract, as are the next four contracts for ship construction. The four contracts for LPD 17 though LPD 20 are overrunning their target prices significantly, as shown in Figure B.4. The contract for LPD 21 was awarded recently and includes some

Figure B.3
DDG 51–Class Shipbuilding Prices per Unit (from SARs)

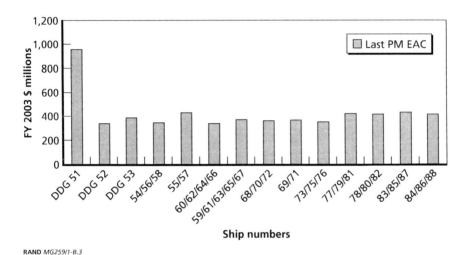

RAND *MG259/1-B.3*

Figure B.4
LPD 17–Class Shipbuilding Prices (from SARs)

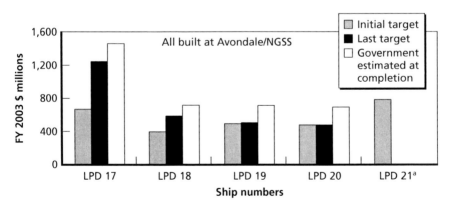

[a]Contract award November 2003.
RAND *MG259/1 B.4*

nonrecurring work. The cost improvement on the four follow ships is not impressive. Ingalls had problems with its design tools, which certainly affected lead ship costs and probably disrupted construction on the concurrent follow ships also. So it is implausible to blame all the poor cost performance on the acquisition strategy alone. Even so, the contrast with performance on the DDG 51 class is striking. The Navy has few options with the LPD 17 program. There are no competitors to whom the Navy can turn to provide incentives for better performance or to complete construction of the class.

Questionnaire for Shipbuilders

RAND sent the following questionnaire to shipbuilders in August 2003. We reproduce it here in its entirety.

RAND Study on the DD(X) for the U.S. Navy

Introduction

The DD(X) Program Office has asked RAND to evaluate Phase IV and beyond acquisition strategies. Evaluation criteria will include cost and schedule, as well as using production capacity efficiently and sustaining the core U.S. surface warship industrial base. As part of the study, we need to obtain basic data on production plans and labor requirements for your firm. We ask that you help us in this study by providing the requested information on the subsequent worksheets. We realize that your firm may consider some of the data proprietary in nature. Accordingly, we are willing to sign a nondisclosure agreement with your firm that would restrict the use of the information that you provide.

Project Monitor

CAPT Charles H. Goddard, USN
DD(X) Program Manager
Naval Sea Systems Command
Washington Navy Yard, D.C.

RAND Principal Investigators

John Birkler	John Schank
Senior Researcher	Senior Operations Research
RAND Corporation	Analyst
1700 Main Street	RAND Corporation
P.O. Box 2138	1200 South Hayes Street
Santa Monica, CA 90407-2138	Arlington, VA 22202-5050
(310) 393-0411, Ext. 7607	(703) 413-1100, Ext. 5304
john_birkler@rand.org	john_schank@rand.org

Directions

Included are additional worksheets requesting data in several different areas. Please complete the worksheets as best you can. If you have questions, please contact one of the principal investigators listed above. Also, please provide contact information for the individuals completing these forms. A space is provided below. If you have supplementary information, please feel free to attach it to this file.

Company Contact Information

Name	Title	Phone	E-Mail

Objective

We wish to obtain an aggregate understanding of past patterns of business activity at individual shipyards involved in production. Here, we ask for employment level as a proxy for the general level of business activity.

Please provide approximate, average employment levels of direct laborers for the entire shipyard each year shown.

Blue-Collar Workers				
Year	Welding	Pipe Fitting	Electrical	Machinery
1990				
1991				
1992				
1993				
1994				
1995				
1996				
1997				
1998				
1999				
2000				
2001				
2002				
2003				

Blue-Collar Workers				
Year	Outfitting	Fitting Fabrication	Construction Support	Other Support
1990				
1991				
1992				
1993				
1994				
1995				
1996				
1997				
1998				
1999				
2000				
2001				
2002				
2003				

White-Collar Workers				
Year	Engineer	Draftsman	Designer	Other
1990				
1991				
1992				
1993				
1994				
1995				
1996				
1997				
1998				
1999				
2000				
2001				
2002				
2003				

Workforce Data

We realize that your firm may use different worker categories. We ask that you please try to fit your categories to ours as best as you can.

Blue-Collar Workers				
Workers Currently Employed	Welding	Pipe Fitting	Electrical	Machinery
Number of Workers				
Average Direct Hourly Wage Rate				
Average Hiring Cost				
Termination Cost				

Blue-Collar Workers				
Workers Currently Employed	Out-fitting	Fitting Fabrication	Construction Support	Other Support
Number of Workers				
Average Direct Hourly Wage Rate				
Average Hiring Cost				
Termination Cost				

White-Collar Workers				
Year	Engineer	Draftsman	Designer	Other
Number of Workers				
Average Direct Hourly Wage Rate				
Average Hiring Cost				
Termination Cost				

Workforce Distribution by Age

Number of workers who are:

Blue-Collar Workers				
Workers Currently Employed	Welding	Pipe Fitting	Electrical	Machinery
Less than 40				
40–50				
50–60				
Greater than 60				

Blue-Collar Workers				
Workers Currently Employed	Out-fitting	Fitting Fabrication	Construction Support	Other Support
Less than 40				
40–50				
50–60				
Greater than 60				

White-Collar Workers				
Year	Engineer	Draftsman	Designer	Other
Less than 40				
40–50				
50–60				
Greater than 60				

Workforce Distribution by Experience

Number of workers with shipbuilding experience of:

Blue-Collar Workers				
Workers Currently Employed	Welding	Pipe Fitting	Electrical	Machinery
Less than 1 year				
1 year				
2 years				
3 years				
4 years				
5 years				
More than 5 years				

Blue-Collar Workers				
Workers Currently Employed	Out-fitting	Fitting Fabrication	Construction Support	Other Support
Less than 1 year				
1 year				
2 years				
3 years				
4 years				
5 years				
More than 5 years				

White-Collar Workers				
Year	Engineer	Draftsman	Designer	Other
Less than 1 year				
1 year				
2 years				
3 years				
4 years				
5 years				
More than 5 years				

What is the standard/average number of hours per year that a full-time employee works? _____

Employment Differences by Experience for Blue-Collar Workers

Year	Attrition Rate (% Annual Loss)	Productivity % (Relative to Highest-Skilled Worker)	Average, Direct Wage Rate ($/hr)	Annual Training Cost
Less than 1 year				
1 year				
2 years				
3 years				
4 years				
5 years				
More than 5 years				

Employment Differences by Experience for White-Collar Workers

Year	Attrition Rate (% Annual Loss)	Productivity % (Relative to Highest-Skilled Worker)	Average, Direct Wage Rate ($/hr)	Annual Training Cost
Less than 1 year				
1 year				
2 years				
3 years				
4 years				
5 years				
More than 5 years				

Training and Hiring of Workers

Please briefly describe the training process for new workers:

Is formal mentoring used? If so, what are the typical ratios between new hires and experienced workers?

If workers have been previously laid off, can they be rehired later? What fraction of the workers can be rehired? For how long? Please describe.

When hiring workers, what are the typical experience levels of the candidate pool?

	Blue-Collar % of total pool	White-Collar % of total pool
Less than one year		
One year		
Two years		
Three years		
Four years		
Five years		
More than five years		

In order to meet peaks in workload, do you employ temporary/contract workers? Please explain:

Initial DD(X) Nonrecurring Workload Profile

Please provide a workload profile for construction of the first-of-class DD(X) destroyer, listing the number of man-hours of direct labor per quarter for each skill. Please list the nonrecurring labor only; use the worksheet title "DD(X) Profile" for recurring labor related to DD(X). We realize that this information is subject to change as the design evolves, please provide your best estimate based on current information. Your firm may use different worker categories—we ask that you please try to fit your categories to ours as best as you can.

Blue-Collar Workers				
Quarter	Welding	Pipe Fitting	Electrical	Machinery
1				
2				
3				
4				
5				
6				
7				
8				
9				
10				
11				
12				
13				
14				
15				
16				
17				
18				
19				
20				
21				
22				
23				
24				
25				
26				
27				
28				
29				
30				
31				
32				

Blue-Collar Workers				
Quarter	Out-fitting	Fitting Fabrication	Construction Support	Other Support
1				
2				
3				
4				
5				
6				
7				
8				
9				
10				
11				
12				
13				
14				
15				
16				
17				
18				
19				
20				
21				
22				
23				
24				
25				
26				
27				
28				
29				
30				
31				
32				

White-Collar Workers				
Quarter	Engineer	Draftsman	Designer	Other
1				
2				
3				
4				
5				
6				
7				
8				
9				
10				
11				
12				
13				
14				
15				
16				
17				
18				
19				
20				
21				
22				
23				
24				
25				
26				
27				
28				
29				
30				
31				
32				

DD(X) Workload Profile

Please provide a workload profile for construction of the first-of-class DD(X) destroyer, listing the number of man-hours of direct labor per quarter for each skill. Please list the recurring labor only, use the worksheet titled "Initial DD(X) Nonrecurring" for nonrecurring labor related to DD(X). We realize that this information is subject to change as the design evolves. Please provide your best estimate based on current information. Your firm may use different worker categories—we ask that you please try to fit your categories to ours as best as you can.

Unit learning curve slope for follow-on ships: _____

Also, indicate quarter in which construction of the item begins and the quarter in which the item is delivered.

Begin Quarter   _____
Delivery Quarter   _____

Blue-Collar Workers				
Quarter	Welding	Pipe Fitting	Electrical	Machinery
1				
2				
3				
4				
5				
6				
7				
8				
9				
10				
11				
12				
13				
14				
15				
16				
17				
18				
19				
20				
21				
22				
23				
24				
25				
26				
27				
28				
29				
30				
31				
32				

Blue-Collar Workers				
Quarter	Out-fitting	Fitting Fabrication	Construction Support	Other Support
1				
2				
3				
4				
5				
6				
7				
8				
9				
10				
11				
12				
13				
14				
15				
16				
17				
18				
19				
20				
21				
22				
23				
24				
25				
26				
27				
28				
29				
30				
31				
32				

White-Collar Workers				
Quarter	Engineer	Draftsman	Designer	Other
1				
2				
3				
4				
5				
6				
7				
8				
9				
10				
11				
12				
13				
14				
15				
16				
17				
18				
19				
20				
21				
22				
23				
24				
25				
26				
27				
28				
29				
30				
31				
32				

Non-DD(X) Production Plans

We would like to have an understanding of your plans for non-DD(X) work.

Model Name (e.g., DDG 51, LPD 17)	Type of work (e.g., new, repair, module)	Start of Engineering Planning (quarter/year)	End of Engineering Planning (quarter/year)	Start of Construction (quarter/year)	End of Construction (quarter/year)	Delivery quarter/year

NOTE: If more than 25 activities are planned, please expand list.

Workload Profile

For each item in the "Non-DD(X) Production Plans" worksheet, please provide a workload profile listing the number of man-hours of direct labor per quarter for each skill. We realize that your firm may use different worker categories. We ask that you please try to fit your categories to ours as best you can.

Unit learning curve slope for follow-on ships: _____

Begin Quarter   _____

Delivery Quarter _____

Blue-Collar Workers				
Quarter	Welding	Pipe Fitting	Electrical	Machinery
1				
2				
3				
4				
5				
6				
7				
8				
9				
10				
11				
12				
13				
14				
15				
16				
17				
18				
19				
20				
21				
22				
23				
24				
25				
26				
27				
28				
29				
30				
31				
32				

Blue-Collar Workers				
Quarter	Out-fitting	Fitting Fabrication	Construction Support	Other Support
1				
2				
3				
4				
5				
6				
7				
8				
9				
10				
11				
12				
13				
14				
15				
16				
17				
18				
19				
20				
21				
22				
23				
24				
25				
26				
27				
28				
29				
30				
31				
32				

White-Collar Workers				
Quarter	Engineer	Draftsman	Designer	Other
1				
2				
3				
4				
5				
6				
7				
8				
9				
10				
11				
12				
13				
14				
15				
16				
17				
18				
19				
20				
21				
22				
23				
24				
25				
26				
27				
28				
29				
30				
31				
32				

Facilities Production Equipment Investments for DD(X) Activities

In order to manufacture DD(X) destroyers, it is possible that your firm may require facilities upgrades, expansions, and the addition of new tooling and equipment. Please itemize descriptions of the improvements and investments needed, assuming that the Navy proceeds with a dual-source contract with your firm for constructing one-half of the planned ships. Please provide all cost values if priced today (i.e., 2003 $).

#	Investment Description	Investment Lead-Time (months)	Completion Date (mo/yr)	Investment Cost ($)	Capitalized or Expensed?	If Expensed, What Is the Depreciation Schedule?
1						
2						
3						
4						
5						
6						
7						
8						
9						
10						
11						
12						
13						
14						
15						
16						
17						
18						
19						
20						

Burden Data

Definition   The term "burden" refers to overhead, general and administrative, fee/profit, and cost of money charges. These costs, which are proportional to the direct hours, are, typically, billed as a percentage of the direct labor hours. Most of this information should be contained in your Forward-Pricing Rate Agreement (FPRA) (if you have one) If possible, please also attach your current FPRA.

What burden/overhead cost pools do you use, what costs are included in each, and how are costs allocated?

Are there burden/overhead costs that are spread to more than one location?

Which do you consider fixed annual costs and which are variable?

Please provide in the table below how burden/overhead changes as a function of the current business base. If you have separate pools for engineering and direct labor, please provide the information for each pool.

% Change in Business Base	Direct Hours	Overhead Rate	General and Administrative Rate	Other _____	Wrap Rate
50%					
40%					
30%					
20%					
10%					
0%					
−10%					
−20%					
−30%					
−40%					
−50%					

Are fringe costs (vacation, health, sick leave, etc.) included in the overhead rate? If not, please provide the current rate as a fraction of the current direct rate.

Direct Labor	Direct Engineering	Other Direct

Do you have a burden rate for cost of money recovery? If so, please provide your current rates.

Direct Labor	Direct Engineering	Other Direct

Please provide an example of how you build up a direct rate to a total wrap rate.

Bibliography

Arena, Mark V., and John F. Schank, *The Shipbuilding and Force Structure Analysis Tool: A User's Guide,* Santa Monica, Calif.: RAND Corporation, MR-1743-NAVY, 2004.

Birkler, J. L., Anthony G. Bower, Jeffrey A. Drezner, Gordon T. Lee, Mark A. Lorell, Giles K. Smith, F. S. Timson, William P. G. Trimble, and Obaid Younossi, *Competition and Innovation in the U.S. Fixed-Wing Military Aircraft Industry,* Santa Monica, Calif.: RAND Corporation, MR-1656-OSD, 2003.

Birkler, J. L., Michael G. Mattock, John F. Schank, Giles K. Smith, Fred Timson, James R. Chiesa, Bruce Woodyard, Malcolm MacKinnon, and Denis Rushworth, *The U.S. Aircraft Carrier Industrial Base: Force Structure, Cost, Schedule, and Technology Issues for CVN 77,* Santa Monica, Calif.: RAND Corporation, MR-948-NAVY/OSD, 1998.

Birkler, J. L., John F. Schank, Mark V. Arena, Giles Smith, and Gordon Lee, *The Royal Navy's New-Generation Type 45 Destroyer: Acquisition Options and Implications,* Santa Monica, Calif.: RAND Corporation, MR-1486-MOD, 2002.

Boger, Dan C., Willis R. Greer, and Shu S. Liao, "Competitive Weapon System Acquisition: Myths and Facts," in Dan C. Boger and Daniel A. Nussbaum, eds., *Competition in Weapon Systems Acquisition: Cost Analysis of Some Issues,* Monterey, Calif.: Naval Postgraduate School, NPS-54-90-021, September 1990.

DD(X) Land Attack Destroyer Single Acquisition Management Plan, Revision D (November 27, 2001). Government publication; not releasable to the general public.

"DDX Media Roundtable," June 30, 2005, briefing.

Department of Defense (DoD), "Acquisition Strategy Proposal: Schedule, Cost, and AP Implications," brief to Kathleen Peroff, Office of Management and Budget, April 27, 2005.

Department of the Navy, Program Executive Office, Ships, *DDG 51 Class Master Planning Schedule,* PEOSHIPSNOTE 4701, OPR 440D3, Ser 400D/212, March 31, 2004.

Goddard, CAPT Chuck, "DD(X) Acquisition Strategy Revision," June 2005.

Lo, T. N., *The Impact of Competition on the CG 47 Construction Program,* Washington, D.C.: Naval Center for Cost Analysis, October 1985.

Memorandum from Principal Deputy Secretary of the Navy (Research Development, and Acquisition), June 5, 1998.

Office of Management and Budget (OMB), Circular No. A-94, *Guidelines and Discount Rates for Benefit-Cost Analysis of Federal Programs,* Washington, D.C., October 1992.

Office of the Secretary of Defense (OSD), Program Decision 753, December 23, 2004.

Pepper, Ranae M., *Effects of Competition on Procurement of TAO 187 Class Ships,* Washington, D.C.: Naval Center for Cost Analysis, January 1989.

Riddick, Rod, "The Aegis Shipbuilding Program," John J. McMullen Associates Web site, available at http://www.jjma.com/Documents/Features/news/aegis.htm, accessed November 2003.

Smith, Giles K., Jeffrey A. Drezner, and Irving Lachow, *Assessing the Use of "Other Transactions" Authority for Prototype Projects,* Santa Monica, Calif.: RAND Corporation, DB-375-OSD, 2002.

Under Secretary of Defense for Acquisition, Technology, and Logistics (USD[AT&L]), "DD(X) Destroyer Acquisition Decision Memorandum," April 20, 2005.

Weisman, Robert, "Raytheon Awarded $3B Navy Contract," *Boston Globe,* May 24, 2005.